To the inquisitive college students of America, who, wherever I have met them, have always asked questions! Especially dear to me are the students of Texas Tech University, Lubbock, Texas, where I served as campus minister for four beautiful years. The hunger of those students to know God's Word caused me to seek the answers to their many questions. May this book enrich your life as they have enriched mine.

Questions
New Christians
Ask

Barry Wood

Fleming H. Revell Company
Old Tappan, New Jersey

Unless otherwise identified, Scripture quotations are from the New American Standard Bible, Copyright © THE LOCKMAN FOUNDATION 1960, 1962, 1963, 1968, 1971, 1972, 1973, 1975 and are used by permission.

Scripture quotations identified KJV are from the King James Version of the Bible.

Scripture quotations identified NEB are from The New English Bible. © The Delegates of the Oxford University Press and the Syndics of the Cambridge University Press 1961 and 1970. Reprinted by permission.

Library of Congress Cataloging in Publication Data

Wood, Barry, date
  Questions new Christians ask.

  Includes bibliographies.
  1. Apologetics—20th century.   I. Title.
BT1102.W64   239   79-20755
ISBN 0-8007-5044-6

Contents

5

Preface

Once a person becomes a born-again Christian, he or she often immediately expects to have all the answers to every problem in life. This just is not true, and many believers become confused by the difficult situations they face. There are answers to their problems, but these answers may not be as obvious as new Christians would like them to be. It takes growth and willingness to change before a believer will be able to solve many questions; but if he knows where to look, he can find the answers when he needs them.

The Bible contains all the information the Christian needs to make the right decisions in the walk of faith. As he turns to God's Word with an open mind and the expectancy that God will enlighten him, the believer will begin to understand more about God and the answers He has provided for every problem. Therefore, I have tried to make the Bible the basis for my answer to each question.

The questions I have chosen to deal with are concerned with Christian growth and maturity. Those who have not taken the first step of faith and accepted Jesus Christ as their personal Saviour will not identify with these problems, but the person who has become a Christian and wants guidance on attaining spiritual maturity will find it a helpful guide.

All the problems a Christian may face cannot possibly be dealt with here, but this book is meant to be a handy one-volume source on some of the confusing issues in Christian life. For those who wish to research any of these issues more thoroughly, I have included a bibliography at the end of each chapter.

I trust that the answers to these questions will be helpful to many who are searching for truth in the midst of confusion. The answers are there, if the believer is willing to search them out.

1 *How Can I Know God's Will?*

An often-asked question which confuses many people is: "How can I know God's will?" As the Christian faces career choices, marriage, and daily decisions, it is crucial that he know how to understand the mind of God on these matters.

F. B. Meyer was once on a ship at sea, coming to port one night. He was standing on the bridge with the captain. It was a very stormy night; and as he looked at the entrance to the harbor, it seemed very narrow. He turned to the captain, on the bridge beside him, and said, "Captain, how do you know when to turn this ship into that narrow harbor?" The captain looked at him and replied, "That's an art. Do you see those three red lights on the shore? When they are all in a straight line, I go right in." God has given us several red lights, or principles, by which we can discern His will for our lives. Often it's only a matter of getting them all in a straight line before we proceed.

Before coming to those principles, there are several insights which should be considered. First, the will of God concerning salvation, morals, and character is universal. It is God's universal will that:

- All people become Christians (2 Peter 3:9; 1 Timothy 2:3, 4)
- All Christians become like Christ (Romans 8:28, 29)
- All Christians be useful (Ephesians 2:10)

God reveals His will concerning Christian service, profession, marriage, and other matters to each believer personally. In Acts 13:2 the Holy Spirit set Paul and Barnabas aside for missionary work. The phrase ". . . except the apostles" in Acts 8:1 indicates that it

9

was God's will for the apostles to serve as ministers in the church in Jerusalem, while laymen were dispersed to carry the Gospel to the far corners of the world (Acts 8:4). This shows us that it's not God's will that all people perform the same task, just as every man cannot marry the same woman. The will of God is individual in many areas of life. He does have an individual plan for you. You can know that and believe it!

So often we forget that God's will is good. God's will is best for us. Satan has deceived us on this point; he has convinced us that if we do God's will, every Monday will be Blue Monday, our lives will be filled with burdens, or God may make us eat worms! Often we treat God's will as though it were an invitation to catch smallpox or to become polluted with leprosy. As one student in Texas told me, "I just know if I surrender to God's will, He'll make me become a Texas Aggie and send me to Africa as a missionary." Not so! God's will is not always spinach! Often it's a banana split! Try it; you'll like it!

Now, when I say God's will is best, I do not mean to imply that it always seems best at the moment. God's will may seem like spinach at the time. If a reporter had asked Job, in the Bible, if he knew those boils were best for him, I feel Brother Job would not have praised the Lord for his afflictions. Yet, later, in hindsight, Job saw the hand of God in it all. We must believe God will do what is best for us— always!

Let's put it this way. Suppose you are a father. One of your sons comes home and says, "Dad, I love you and Mom so much that I am going to put my life in your hands. I am going to let you do anything you want to do with me today." You say, "Excuse me just a minute, son." You go into the bedroom, where your wife is, and say, "Honey, I just heard the best news. Our son has said he loves us so much that he is going to put his life in our hands, and today we can do anything we want to do with him. Get a pencil and paper and write down all those things that will make his life miserable, unhappy, and unfruitful." No, you wouldn't do that. You would say, "Honey, let's see what we can do to make our son's life meaningful, happy, and fruitful."

In a like manner, whenever we put our lives in the hands of God to do His will, He will give us the best in life. He gives us freedom and abundant life. He gives each Christian direction for right decisions, such as which college to attend, who to marry, what vocation to follow, and the best church in which to serve Christ and others.

The Unsaved and God's Will

Before we can understand these truths, we must realize that there are two types of people in our world, and they relate to this problem in completely different ways. There are saved people and lost people. Lost people cannot expect God to reveal His will to them. There is no communion between God and the lost, and usually the lost person is not even interested in knowing God's will. To know God's will, one must come to Jesus in a commitment of faith and repentance. Once you become God's child, you can be guided by Him as your Father. The Lord said in John 10:3, ". . . he calleth his own sheep by name, and leadeth them out" (KJV). God's will begins, for you, the moment Jesus comes into your life. God's first plan for you is that you be saved. The Christian can expect God to reveal His will. God's will is not some hidden secret which must be discovered. Usually the problem in discovering God's purpose lies with us, not Him. Christians usually fall into one of three categories:

- Some Christians are not concerned about knowing God's will
- Some Christians want to know His will, but are not willing to pay the price
- Some Christians want to know God's will and are willing to take the necessary steps

What is your attitude toward the plan of God for your life?

You Must Want God's Will

Jesus desired to do God's will. In His most crucial hour of testing He prayed, ". . . Father . . . not as I will, but as Thou wilt" (Matthew 26:39). Our Lord taught us to pray, "Thy kingdom come. Thy will be done, On earth as it is in heaven" (Matthew 6:10). Now, do you want God's will on earth to start with you? Do you desire His will? That is the first step in knowing God's will.

God wants you to know His will. ". . . we have not ceased to pray for you and to ask that you may be filled with the knowledge of His will in all spiritual wisdom and understanding" (Colossians 1:9). This is exciting! God desires that you know His plan for your life. God's will is not a big Easter-egg hunt. He wants you to be filled with the knowledge of His will. You don't have to seek His will, because God will reveal it to you, if you want to know it.

Suppose I were to call in my child and say, "I have something I want you to do, and if you don't do it, I'll spank you." My child says, "Okay, Dad, what is it you want me to do?" I reply, "I'm not going to tell you! You've got to guess, and if you miss it, I'm going to spank you!" Many people act as though that's how God treats us!

Scriptural Guidelines

The Scriptures tell us some basic truths about God's will and purpose for our lives. We need to know these things to help us desire His will to be done in us:

God does have a plan for us. Ephesians 1:9, 11 says, "He made known to us the mystery of His will . . . having been predestined according to His purpose who works all things after the counsel of His will." That's great! God has a special plan for every Christian. He knows me! Jesus said every hair on my head is numbered by God.

God's plan is a good one. Paul says the will of God is ". . . good and acceptable and perfect" (Romans 12:2). I need to want His will, because it fits me perfectly.

God's plan has basic guidelines. Before I can experience God's daily guidance I need to know some fundamental scriptural principles regarding God's will. God's plan for me will always be in keeping with these principles.

What are some of these guidelines? The details of God's plan will never contradict these five universal principles:

- God's will is your sanctification. "For this is the will of God . . . that is, that you abstain from sexual immorality" (1 Thessalonians 4:3). God wants you to be sexually pure.

- God's will is your continual thanksgiving. "In everything give thanks; for this is God's will for you in Christ Jesus" (1 Thessalonians 5:18). He wants you to praise Him in everything—good and bad.
- God's will is for you to do right, because this silences ignorant men. First Peter 2:15 says, "For such is the will of God that by doing right you may silence the ignorance of foolish men." He wants your life to be above reproach, that others might see Jesus in you.
- God's will is that you should sometimes have a difficult time. First Peter 4:19 says, "Therefore, let those who suffer according to the will of God entrust their souls to a faithful Creator in doing what is right." Often God wants us to suffer for Him, to develop faith and character in us.
- God's will is for you to be glorified with Him. "And if children, heirs also, heirs of God and fellow-heirs with Christ, if indeed we suffer with Him in order that we may also be glorified with Him" (Romans 8:17).

Several years ago I led a young ex-sailor to Christ. A few months later he told me God was leading him to go to school to train to become a bartender. I told him I thought he was mistaken. God wouldn't lead him to do that. I had him consider these five scriptural guidelines. I told him God's will would never violate or contradict these principles. After prayerful consideration, he realized it was not God's will for him to serve drinks.

Do You Really Want His Will?

Often when we read these guidelines, we know God's will in our minds, but we lack the will to obey. Paul tells us in Ephesians 5:17: "So then do not be foolish, but understand what the will of the Lord is." Knowing God's will and understanding it are not always the same thing. Understanding comes only when we obey the will of God. God's will must get into our hearts, not just our heads. Often we know what the Father wants and have no intention of doing it! True availability to do His will is often the key. When we truly want

His will to be done, He fills our hearts with the knowledge of His will.

Recently a college person came to my office, wanting some guidance for the future. As this student talked, two things became very clear to me. First, God had obviously been leading this student to make a commitment to a full-time Christian vocation. God had closed several doors to other opportunities and had revealed His will in the direction of Christian work. A second thing was also clear to me. This student did not want to do the will of God, even though he said he did. Because of his unwillingness, he just couldn't see God's leading. Availability is the key!

Working Out His Will

When the believer desires His will, how does he then discover it? How does he know exactly what to do in given situations—not in the sweet by and by, but in the dirty here and now! Paul challenged the believer to prove that God's plan is ". . . good and acceptable and perfect." How do I go about proving it?

Yielding to God. Notice the condition for discovering God's will. In Romans 12:1, 2 Paul tells us to present ourselves totally to God and to be transformed in the renewing of our minds. What he is saying is simply this: A yielded life opens the door to God's daily guidance. My spiritual condition must be right if I am to discern God's leadership. Those who are Spirit-filled Christians are also Spirit-led Christians, because they are alert to the mind of God.

Putting out a fleece. I am often asked, "What do you think about putting out a fleece?" This question is a reference to the experience in the life of Gideon when he sought to know God's will by giving God a test (Judges 6). Since that time, a fleece has come to mean a type of divining rod for knowing God's will. Suppose you want to know if God wants you to take a certain job tomorrow. All right, you give God a fleece. You say, "God, if it doesn't rain tomorrow morning, I'll take that as a sign that you want me to have that job; and I'll take it." Is this a valid method? Well, as I've said, God's will works along biblical guidelines, and He doesn't usually send out smoke signals or flashing lights. He usually lets us know His will and way when we are sensitive to His Word and His Spirit. He speaks to the inner man. First Corinthians 2:10 says, "For to us God revealed them [His will] through the Spirit . . . ." I would think that putting out a fleece would be helpful only as a last resort, and only then after much prayer and searching!

Condition and promise. Those Christians who seem to always know and do the will of the Lord are those people who meet His conditions for a walk of faith. Proverbs 3:5, 6 is a good illustration. These verses contain three conditions and one promise:

- Trust in the Lord with all your heart,
- And do not lean on your own understanding.
- In all your ways acknowledge Him . . . .

After these conditions comes the promise, ". . . And He will make your paths straight."

If you are fulfilling the conditions and claiming the promise, you won't make a mistake. *He* is responsible to direct your path.

Our Part and His

Have you noticed that, when we don't know which way to go, we often stick our nose into God's part and neglect ours? God says we are to

Trust in Him

In every way acknowledge Him

Do not lean on our own wisdom

Then He will do His part. It's not our job to keep checking up on God. We must fulfill the conditions of faith, and it is His responsibility to work it out.

Making Daily Decisions

It may sound silly, but you don't have to pray about what color clothes you wear, how you'll style your hair, and so forth. Simply keep an attitude of trust and availability, seeking to walk in obedience. Then God will give you His impressions for your daily needs. Also, doing God's will is not a matter of sitting around doing nothing and calling it waiting on the Lord. Waiting on the Lord means to move along in an attitude of dependence and availability. Don't wait for a green light, but keep moving until you get a red light. Walk through doors until God slams one shut in front of you.

Making Major Decisions

Having given many guidelines, now let's come down to some very practical aids for determining God's will when major decisions have to be made.

- *Consider your convictions.* Does this decision agree with your biblically based convictions? Is it contrary to conscience?
- *Consider your circumstances.* Do your circumstances match your convictions? Suppose you have a conviction that God wants you to be a singer, but you are tone deaf! It doesn't seem likely that God would lead you in that direction.
- *Seek the advice of many people.* God has deposited His wisdom in the lives of those who have lived out His will. He can lead you through their counsel.
- *Let the Scriptures be your guide.* Suppose you are trying to decide whether or not you should commit suicide. That's a rather major decision! If you decide wrongly, you won't get a second chance! Beware of pulling verses out of context. For example, you read:

  "Judas went out and hanged himself."
  "Go thou and do likewise."
  "What thou doest, do quickly."

That kind of Scripture study can lead you astray! Be careful to search the Scriptures wisely to gain insight and advice on your decision.
- *Determine not to make a major decision until these all jibe.* When there is a doubt, you have to step out on faith and see how God leads. At this point, a reasonable fleece might be helpful.

Common Mistakes to Avoid

Paul Little, in his pamphlet entitled *Affirming the Will of God,* set out several common mistakes that should be avoided in seeking

God's will. Here are some misrepresentations of God's attitude that are prevalent among believers.

- Do not think that because you want to do something, it can't possibly be God's will.
- Do not feel that every decision you make must have a subjective confirmation. Some people have become paralyzed and could not act because they did not have an electrifying shiver about their proposed course of action.
- Realize that there are logical implications involved in the will of God. If God leads you to get married, you do not have to spend hours in prayer, agonizing over whether or not it is the will of God for you to support your family.
- Do not think that God's will is necessarily something wild and bizarre.
- Guard carefully against the subtle temptation to decide what you are going to do for God. This is a critical mistake. There is a vast difference between saying, "Lord, I am going to be a businessman for You," and asking, "Lord, what would You have me to do?"
- Guard against the temptation to take Bible verses out of context to try to get God's will.
- Avoid the idea that you can be sure you are in the will of God if everything is moonlight and roses, if you have no problems or stress. The test of whether or not you are in the will of God is not how rosy your circumstances are, but whether or not you are obeying Him.
- Avoid the mistake of thinking that a call to world evangelism or to missionary service is any different from a call to anything else. The crucial question is, "Am I in the will of God, and am I sure of it?"
- Avoid the mistake of thinking that if you have ever knowingly and willingly disobeyed the Lord, you are forever thrown on the ash heap; you can never do the Lord's will; and you are doomed to second best. This is just not so!

Additional Reading

Barnette, Henlee. *Has God Called You?* Nashville: Broadman
    Press, 1969.

Little, Paul. *Affirming the Will of God.* Downers Grove, IL: Inter-
    Varsity Press.

Maston, Thomas B. *God's Will and Your Life.* Nashville: Broadman
    Press, 1964.

Pinson, William M. *The Will of God.* Nashville: Broadman Press,
    1974.

Trueblood, Elton. *Your Other Vocation.* New York: Harper & Row,
    1952.

Weatherhead, Leslie D. *The Will of God.* Nashville: Abingdon
    Press, 1974.

2 Right or Wrong: How Can I Decide?

Life is a journey of many decisions. Every day of our lives we come to crossroads and have to decide which path we will take. The final result—the success or failure of our lives—will be determined by those little decisions we make along the way. Therefore, a vital question for the believer is: "How do I make moral choices?"

What Does the Bible Say?

The Bible can help us make the right decisions; but in order to consider the principles it gives us, we must consider the attitude we have toward the Bible itself. Do you accept the sovereignty of God's will, as revealed in His Word? Are you willing to submit your decisions to this final test: What does God say in His Holy Scripture? If you are willing to do these things, you need never make a wrong moral decision.

In making a moral choice based on Scripture, we must be aware of some principles about using the Bible to find direction for our lives. First, the Bible is a guidebook, not a rule book. Often believers will look for specific directives such as, "Thou shalt not smoke cigarettes," and so forth. The Bible wasn't meant to be used that way, though, and this legalistic attitude can destroy the believer's freedom in the Spirit. Second Corinthians 3:17 tell us that the Holy Spirit is the Spirit of freedom.

Others will try to go in another direction, and when specific directives do not exist, they will try to use that as an excuse to do as they

19

please. Some people have said, "Well, the Bible doesn't condemn smoking marijuana. Therefore it must be okay." Some have reasoned, "I want a specific law or rule, so I will know exactly what is right or wrong." Such reasoning is faulty. The Bible wasn't meant to be used that way, either. If God had said centuries ago, "Thou shalt not smoke marijuana," the result would have been that no one in Moses' community of exiled Jews would have known what marijuana was; and, from that time forward, they would have been curious to find out what it was, so they could smoke some of it! That's human nature. Our sinful nature will nearly always rebel against rules and regulations. Those who make the Bible a rule book are inviting this legalistic approach to life.

Although we should be careful about rules, legalism should not be confused with the specific, clear directives which are God's timeless laws. The Bible says, "Thou shalt not steal," and, "Thou shalt not bear false witness." There should be little disagreement in the meaning of these commandments, and they are truths to live by.

But what of places in which God's commandments are not so flatly stated? How can the believer know how to do the right thing? God does not give specific directives on everything in the Christian life. He generally gives us principles rather than rules and regulations. These principles have no exceptions. They are God's road signs to guide us on life's pathway. They are timeless and always relevant to our situations. Every moral, ethical, social, or spiritual decision we ever make can be guided by these principles. A principle is the *why* behind God's laws. We can apply them to all our moral choices.

As much as is humanly possible, I have tried to submit my personal opinions to the authority of Scripture. I hope you will do the same. God has not left us without an answer. His Word speaks to all life's issues. Like nuggets of gold, His truth is there, lying buried in His Word. We must dig it out.

Seven Eternal Principles

The number *seven* in Scripture is a very sacred number, symbolizing completeness. So, let's apply seven biblical guidelines, or principles, to these commonly asked questions. I'm sure there are others, but seven is a good number and will give us ample light to brighten our pathway. Let's look at God's guidelines for determining right from wrong.

Is THERE A DIRECT COMMAND FROM GOD ON THE MATTER? Sometimes God has spoken directly to a moral question. Some activities are always wrong, regardless of the situation. For example, the Ten Commandments are eternal laws. There is never a right time to lie, murder, or covet.[1]

Suppose a Christian girl wants to marry a lost guy. God has an absolute commandment for us on this matter. The Apostle Paul said he had a word from the Lord forbidding such a marriage. The apostle writes, "Do not unite yourselves with unbelievers; they are no fit mates for you. What has righteousness to do with wickedness? . . ." (2 Corinthians 6:14 NEB). That's plain enough, isn't it? The Apostle Paul tells us it is never God's perfect will for a Christian to be "unequally yoked together" in marriage with a lost person. This does not mean such marriages are unholy unions. It simply means God has given clear instruction on this matter, and we should not disobey. A rather extensive discussion of this subject is given in chapter eleven.

DOES THIS GLORIFY GOD? Here is our second guideline for making moral choices. The Apostle Paul writes in 1 Corinthians 10:31, "Whether, then, you eat or drink or whatever you do, do all to the glory of God."

This is a fundamental Christian principle. Can God be glorified in your actions? Will Jesus Christ be magnified in this activity? We are God's mirrors to reflect Jesus to the world. We are Christ's ambassadors. We represent the King.

This matter of glorifying God is another way of asking what Jesus would do in this situation. You see, many things are not evil in and of themselves, but our motivation can be wrong. An illustration might be helpful here. Do you consider prayer to be a virtuous activity? Well, it should be, but it can be used selfishly. In Luke 18:10–14, the Lord Jesus told of two men who went to the temple to pray. One of them, a sinful yet humble tax collector, prayed a prayer that God honored. He asked God to grant him forgiveness for his sins. Such praying glorifies God. The other fellow, a self-centered, self-righteous Pharisee, prayed a prayer that glorified himself, not God.

By such praying he turned a virtuous deed into a sinful act. His motivation was wrong.

As a Christian faces moral choices throughout each day, he needs to keep this basic principle in mind. Submit each decision to the "motive test," remembering Paul's words, "Whether, then, you eat or drink or whatever you do, do all to the glory of God" (1 Corinthians 10:31).

In Colossians 3:17, Paul encourages us again, "And whatever you do in word or deed, do all in the name of the Lord Jesus, giving thanks through Him to God the Father."

Can God be glorified in this? Can I do it in the name of the Lord Jesus? Can I thank Him for it afterward? These questions can help the believer find God's will when facing activities such as the books he reads, the movies he sees, or places of amusement he attends.

Is It a Cause of Stumbling for Others? A third and vital principle has to do with the Christian's responsibility toward other people. First Corinthians 8:13 expresses this thought very well: "Therefore, if food causes my brother to stumble, I will never eat meat again, that I might not cause my brother to stumble." Also, Romans 14:21 says, "It is good not to eat meat or drink wine, or to do anything by which your brother stumbles."

Do I offend others? Perhaps the greatest Christian of the early Church, the Apostle Paul, was very careful what he did, lest he offend his fellowman and thus bring reproach on his Saviour. The eighth chapter of 1 Corinthians contains Paul's thoughts on actions which may offend others. Paul illustrates this point by using the example of eating meat that had been used as a sacrifice on a pagan altar. The problem arose because Gentile Christians were buying used meat in the marketplace. The meat was cheaper, but it had been used as a sacrifice to an idol in a pagan temple. The Jewish Christians in the Corinthian church were appalled at this practice. They were deeply offended, thinking this to be a sin. As Jews, they had been taught that such food had been contaminated, and to a Jewish Christian it was immoral to eat such meat. This practice was causing division in the fellowship.

The apostle says three things about this issue:

- There was essentially nothing wrong with the meat itself. The idol had not contaminated such meat.
- The Christian could eat such meat, unless it became an offense to the conscience of his Christian brother.
- Therefore, ". . . I will never eat meat offered to idols again, that I might not cause my brother to stumble." He says again in 1 Corinthians 10:25, "Eat anything that is sold in the meat market, without asking questions for conscience' sake." In verse 29 he explains, "I mean not your own conscience, but the other man's . . . ."

The point here is that some things may not be wrong in themselves, but for the sake of others who may not be as free in Christ as you are, you should not do it.

His weakness, my chains. But how far do we go in giving up our freedom for another man's conscience? Paul says, "But take care lest this liberty of yours somehow become a stumbling block to the weak" (1 Corinthians 8:9). All right, how much care must I take, and how much freedom must I give up? Must I be continually giving up my freedom in Christ for another's conscience' sake? [2] As a preacher and pastor, I have personally struggled with this question many times. There are those who have a very strict code of ethics set up for the clergy that they do not require of ordinary Christians. For example, can a preacher go to a movie without offending at least somebody, or can he play golf on Sunday afternoon? There may be nothing immoral about the movie, and there certainly is freedom to play golf on Sunday but what if someone is offended? [3] Frequently a lost person takes great delight in "catching" a Christian in some act he considers inappropriate, when in reality the activity may be quite innocent. I have had to struggle with this problem many times.

It seems to me the principles of love and common sense are helpful here. If I am made aware that I have offended someone by my freedom in Christ, my first responsibility is to go to that person and apologize to him. Then I can seek to explain my feelings regarding the activity that was offensive to him. It is possible that God will use my enlightened conscience to give instruction to this weaker brother and thereby contribute to his growth. It is also possible that the so-called weaker brother or sister may contribute to my growth by showing me that I have turned liberty into license. I may find out that I am the weaker one of the two! Many times God has used the conscience of others to show me areas of sin in my life.

Having explained my feelings, should the offended person still not allow my freedom, it is then my responsibility "not to eat meat" in my brother's presence. This does not mean I give up my freedom, but rather that I seek to avoid offending others whenever possible.

Love versus freedom. When I was a senior in high school, God showed me this principle in real life. I was working afternoons at a major meat-packing plant in our city. Most of the men I worked with were not Christians. Two fellows in particular continuously gave me a hard time. They enjoyed needling me and calling me "preacher boy." One day a discussion came up about right and wrong. Being heavy drinkers, these unsaved men were seeking to justify their frequent drunkenness on weekends. One of them said to me, "What's the difference between having a beer and drinking a Coke? A beer is better for your health than a Coke. Why, preacher, you drink a Coke every day for lunch."

Now, granted, his reasoning was a bit way-out, but I asked him if he really meant what he said. I asked, "Are you saying that my drinking a Coke for lunch qualifies you to get drunk? Because if that is what you are saying, I'll never drink another Coke on the job." And I didn't! In fact, a week or so later one of those men came to me and apologized for putting me down for drinking a Coke. Then he proceeded to admit he was ashamed of his drunkenness. I eventually won that fellow to Christ. His salvation was worth giving up a few Cokes! Don't you agree?

IS THIS ACTIVITY NECESSARY? Is this action really needful? First Corinthians 6:12 concludes, "All things are lawful for me, but not all things are profitable . . . ." Also, Paul says in 1 Corinthians 10:23, 24, ". . . All things are lawful, but not all things edify. Let no one seek his own good, but that of his neighbor."

Now what is this principle? Many activities are lawful for us, but are not necessary. We can do without them, if others are going to be hurt by our freedom.

For instance, is it permitted for a Christian to drink coffee or tea? Yes, I think it is, but what if, during the lunch hour, you are talking about Jesus to a Mormon? I suggest you give up your freedom and not drink these beverages while in his presence. To not drink coffee for your Mormon friend's sake does not mean coffee is wrong to drink all the time.

Can a preacher play golf on Sunday? Maybe—there is nothing wrong with recreation on Sunday. The Lord's Day is for our enjoyment. However, if his community is blind to this liberty, he should postpone this activity until another day. According to 1 Corinthians 10:24, out of love for others, we can do without some things.

DOES IT HARM THE BODY OR ROB MY FREEDOM? First Corinthians 3:16, 17 tells us, "Do you not know that you are a temple of God, and that the Spirit of God dwells in you? If any man destroys the temple of God, God will destroy him, for the temple of God is holy . . . ."

Our body belongs to Jesus. We are to use it for His honor and glory. I am not to harm my body. This is sin. Anything that is destructive to my body offends God.

Is alcohol harmful to the body? The answer to that question depends upon whom you ask. In his new book, *Why Drinking Can Be Good for You*, Dr. Morris Chafetz says a drink a day can keep the doctor away! Dr. Chafetz, who is now president of the Health Education Foundation in Washington, recommends a daily consumption of no more than one and a half ounces of pure alcohol, daily. He says it helps prevent heart disease. Now that is news! For years now the medical community has been teaching that any traceable part of alcohol in the bloodstream is harmful to our physical well-being. According to most authorities, alcohol destroys brain cells, causes heart problems, and damages the liver.[4] All right, who is right? Millions of Christians are confused about social drinking. Is it a sin or not? This much is sure: Any activity that is harmful to your body displeases our heavenly Father. This is why He forbids excessive drinking to the point of drunkenness (Ephesians 5:18). The Christian who wants to please God must apply this principle, along with several others, and let the Spirit of God lead him to a conclusion.

Is it addictive? Another guideline is expressed in 1 Corinthians 6:12: "All things are lawful for me, but not all things are profitable. All things are lawful for me, but I will not be mastered by anything." Paul says he only wants one master in his life: Jesus. He wants nothing else to control or master him.

For example, many physical appetites can enslave us. Food is good, but overindulgence and bondage to food or drink is sin.

DOES THIS ACTIVITY PROMOTE EVIL? Romans 12:9 admonishes us to ". . . Abhor what is evil . . . ." First Thessalonians 5:22 tells us to "abstain from every form of evil." Jesus said, "The good man out of his good treasure brings forth what is good; and the evil man out of his evil treasure brings forth what is evil" (Matthew 12:35).

Christians cannot, in good conscience, promote evil. Often we are advancing Satan's kingdom unconsciously, and this is unfortunate. However, we must not knowingly give our money or consent to those activities or agencies that promote evil.

For example, the liquor industry is a very rich and powerful force for evil. It promotes, by its very product, alcoholism, divorce, murder, lust, and violence. A Christian should ask, "Am I promoting and endorsing evil when I purchase liquor?"

This principle could be applied to many other moral choices as well. We each must prayerfully examine our own heart.

CAN I ASK GOD'S BLESSING ON IT? In deciding what is right or wrong, we must submit each question to this seven-fold test. Our final principle is based upon the previous six. If, after applying these principles, I can pray about my moral choice and ask God to bless it, and if I get a *yes* answer down in my spirit, then I can proceed.

Apply these principles; tell God your desire to do His will; and you are not likely to go wrong.[5]

Now let's see if it works. Can a Christian prayerfully submit a contemporary moral choice to this seven-fold test and get a word from the Lord? Well, it's worth a try! A current craze in America is disco dancing. Young people and adults have gone bananas over the

Saturday Night Fever. Can a Christian participate in disco dancing at the local spot? Suppose a Christian couple are on a date. They consider going dancing at a popular disco nightclub. Is this activity pleasing to God? Let's ask some questions about it.

Is there a direct command from God on disco dancing? Obviously there is not! In fact, he tells us to praise Him in the dance. Dancing is not wrong in itself.

Is my motive for dancing to glorify God? Not all dancing can glorify God. Salome danced her lewd, sensual dance before Herod and enticed him to kill John the Baptist. Both Herod and John lost their heads over Salome's dance!

What about the motive? Some would say disco is just plain fun and good exercise. This may be true, but is this type of dancing sensual? Most guys will admit disco is very sexy. It can create sexual lust in both the guy and the girl.

Does the music glorify God? Or does it, too, arouse sensual passions? Romans 8:6 says, "For the mind set on the flesh is death . . . ." Much disco music does tend to set the mind on the flesh. It can create sensual appetites.

Is it a source of stumbling to others? What about their Christian witness? Will it be hurt by dancing in such a place? Could they share Christ with someone there? (I doubt if He could hear them above the noise!)

Is this activity expedient? Do we *have* to go there? If it is doubtful as to whether we should go, then perhaps we can do without it.

Would we be promoting evil? Here is a valuable fact to consider. Would we be promoting or condoning evil by paying money to go to such a place? By going, are we consenting to much evil that goes on there, whether we participate in it or not (such as drugs, drunkenness, lust, and so on)?

Does it harm our bodies? Well, no, not unless you're out of shape and have a stroke right there on the spot! That could be hazardous to your health and harmful to your pride!

Can we ask God's blessing on it? I wonder if a couple in a disco club could bow their heads and pray this prayer, "Father, bless us tonight as we dance, turn each other on, enjoy this atmosphere, and otherwise glorify You by being in this place tonight. Amen." I don't think I could, and I love music and believe some dancing is honorable! But then, that's my conviction. I do know that if any one born-again believer will sincerely apply these principles to any given situation, that our Father will speak to that person and reveal His will.

Source Notes

1. Joseph Fletcher, in his book *Situation Ethics: The New Morality* (Philadelphia: Westminster Press, 1966) would take exception to this principle. Fletcher's approach to moral decisions says there is only one principle: the Love Principle. He says we have only one question to ask: Is it the loving thing to do?
2. By *liberty* I mean my freedom in Christ: those activities I feel free to participate in without a sense of guilt or conviction. The Christian's liberty encompasses all those things God's Spirit has sanctified in his own individual conscience, based upon the Word.
3. Some believers have sought to turn the Lord's Day, Sunday, into the Jewish sabbath, with all its legalistic trappings. Sunday is the believer's day of celebration of a risen Lord, as well as a day free from work.
4. Joel Fort, *Alcohol: Our Biggest Drug Problem* (New York: McGraw-Hill, 1973). *See* chapter two: "The Effects of Alcohol on the Body."
   See also Albion Roy King, *Basic Information on Alcohol* (Washington DC: Narcotics Education, Inc., 1953), pp. 82–93.
5. T. B. Maston and William M. Pinson, Jr., *Right or Wrong?* (Nashville: Broadman Press, 1955).

Additional Reading

Fry, Thomas A., Jr. *Get Off the Fence!* Old Tappan, NJ: Fleming H. Revell, 1963.
Maston, T. B., and Pinson, William M. *Right or Wrong?* Nashville: Broadman Press, 1955.
Ridenour, Fritz. *It All Depends*. Glendale, CA: Regal Books, 1969.
Schlink, M. Basilea. *And None Would Believe It*. Grand Rapids: Zondervan, 1967.

3 Are All Church Members Born Again?

"Are you a born-again Christian?" This question, which used to be very rare, is now heard quite frequently. The term *born again* has been glamorized by the press and media, and recently such books as *Born Again* and *How to Be Born Again* have alerted the world to this Christian experience.[1] The film *Born Again* has excited much interest, and major television networks have run special shows investigating this phenomenon. Celebrities are announcing "I've been born again." People all over the world are finding it acceptable to identify with Jesus Christ as one of His born-again followers.

One of the results of this media exposure is a growing confusion among millions of faithful churchgoers who have never even heard the term before. What does it mean to be born again, and why haven't we all been told about it?

Is This Trip Necessary?

There are multitudes of average churchgoers happily testifying that they are Christians, who haven't a clue about what it is to be born again. They might reply to questions about this that it is not a part of their dogma. Many of them probably view the born-again movement as strange and slightly fanatical.

Many of these people are probably much like Nicodemus, a Jewish rabbi who came to visit Jesus late one evening. He was a devout man, a man of letters, power, and political prestige; he had come to the Carpenter with this in mind: "I have heard You are a

29

teacher come from God; could You teach me about Him?'' In His
response, Jesus did not stop to debate the nature of the universe or
prove God's existence; He went to the heart of the matter, saying,
''Unless you are born again, you can never get into the kingdom of
God'' (John 3:3 author's paraphrase). Nicodemus was as astonished
at this statement as any religious person today could be. Nicodemus
thought he was already a part of the kingdom of God because of his
moral life and his attempts to follow all the rules of the Law. He
exclaimed, ''Born again? What do you mean? How can an old man
like myself go back into his mother's womb and be born a second
time?'' (John 3:4 author's paraphrase.) Perhaps that's what you
would have said. I recently met a college student from South
America. I asked her if she was a Christian, to which she replied,
''Yes.'' I asked her if she had been born again; she was
dumbfounded. She had never heard of such a thing.

Many modern-day believers are just like that. Many of them are
astonished at the statement that they must be born again. They can
understand going to church, trying to live a moral life, paying their
bills, obeying the law, or giving money to charity. However, when
you begin talking about being born again as being essential to real
Christianity, they stop and stare at you like a calf staring at a new
gate!

To some people, preachers who preach ''you must be born again''
are good people, but a little off above the collar button—perfectly
harmless, but they have a slight case of religious insanity! Now it's
important that we understand a fundamental truth. Jesus said, ''you
must be born again'' (John 3:17), and He said it to a man who didn't
know he needed it! Jesus, our Lord, would have us know that born-
again Christianity is the only real kind of Christianity there is. This
new-birth experience is not for a few elite people who happen to
have found a new or different way to God. The new birth is the only
way to God. There is only one door to heaven, and that is by way of
being born again. It is a must. It is not optional equipment.

BORN AGAIN? All right, what is this experience of being born again?
Just as the well-trained religious rabbi Nicodemus did not understand, many today do not understand. Nicodemus thought Jesus
was referring to a second physical birth (John 3:4). Jesus explained

to him that the new birth to which He referred was not a physical rebirth, but rather a spiritual rebirth. It means a change in a person's inner being, a change of our basic nature. Being born again carries the idea of being born from above. The Greek word for *again* that Jesus used means "from above." What Jesus meant was that we all need a rebirth in our characters, and only God can do that. We must have a new nature and be born of the Spirit of God.

The Heart of the Problem!

Perhaps you are wondering why this is so important. Well, it has to do with what's really wrong with our world and what will really cure its ills. For years now sociologists and other men of science have been trying to improve our world. Through knowledge, science, invention, discovery, philosophy, and materialistic advances, we have sought to improve the life of mankind upon this planet. Many advances have been made and many things have been made better. In fact, everything seems to improve—except man himself. In our essential moral nature, which governs our relationship to our fellowman, modern man continues to steal, murder, lie, cheat, and grab. Little of human nature has changed since the beginning of time. The newspaper accounts of rape, murder, brutality, and runaway crime indicate that somewhere we have failed.

Carl Jung, the great psychologist, said, "All the old primitive sins are not dead, but are crawling in the dark corners of our modern heart . . . still there, and still as ghastly as ever."

The famous statesman-publisher Walter Lippman said:

> We ourselves were so sure that at long last a generation had arisen, keen and eager, to put this disorderly earth to right . . . and fit to do it . . . we meant so well, we tried so hard, and look what we have made of it. We can only muddle in muddle. What is required is a new kind of man.

Dag Hammarskjöld, president of the United Nations General Assembly, said twenty years ago: "I see no hope for world peace. We have tried so hard and we have failed so miserably. Unless the world has a spiritual rebirth within the next few years, civilization as we know it is doomed."

What is the solution to this problem? How do we change man for good? Can man change himself?

CHANGE THE ENVIRONMENT. Many sociologists think all that is needed is to change our environment. They say sin is external, not internal. Man is all right; it's his environment that is wrong. They say sin is imaginary, and man is simply a product of bad circumstances. Thus, a juvenile delinquent is merely underprivileged, and a robber is simply maladjusted. In this philosophy we abandon the idea of sin and individual responsibility and blame everything but the offender. Therefore, all that is wrong with the world can be explained in terms of bad housing, slums, racial discrimination, poverty, and unemployment, while the real offender—man himself—remains untouched and unchanged.

CHANGING THE INNER MAN. Could it be that they are wrong? I think so. The Bible teaches us we all need a new nature to change our inner being, because our inner being is sinful, selfish, and godless (Romans 5:12, 19). Man's problem is not *where* he is, but *what* he is. I do what I do because I am what I am. I commit sins because I am a sinner at heart. Therefore, to stop me from sinning, you must change my heart. That's why Jesus said, "You must be born of the Spirit."

REGENERATION OR REFORMATION? If what is needed is an inner change, how does this spiritual rebirth take place? Does church membership or baptism provide this new birth? No, it does not. Jesus addressed this challenge of the new birth to a very moral, religious man. But morality is not the new birth. The new birth Jesus offers provides something better than morality; it provides spirituality. Morality means right relations with your fellowman; spirituality means right relations with God. Not every moral person is a spiritual person. You only become a spiritual person when you are born of the Spirit—the Holy Spirit. When one is born from above, God's very life is implanted in him. This new birth is not reformation, that is, our trying to do better or turn over a new leaf. It is not outward but inward. It's something God does in us, not something we do for Him. It's a divine regeneration, rather than human reformation.

It's Hard to Define

Just what is this born-again experience that puts us in fellowship with God and changes our inner being? Trying to define or explain this spiritual birth Jesus said we all must have is like trying to explain the wind. Indeed, that's how Jesus described it—like the wind (John 3:8). It is a mysterious, wonderful work of God in us.

Yet someone has defined the new birth this way: To be born again is to have a personal experience of conversion to Jesus Christ. However, this definition only describes what it means to be born again; it does not explain it.

Why Wasn't I Told?

A personal experience of conversion to Jesus Christ: That's what Jesus said is a must in everyone's life before he can see the Kingdom of God. A college student said to me a few years ago, "If I have to be born again to be a Christian, why wasn't I told this before now?" That's a reasonable question. It's a remarkable thing that millions of sincere people can go to church all their lives, seeking to know God in Christ, and never be told how to be born again. It is a tragic indictment against ministers that people can come to church like beggars seeking bread, and the minister hands them a stone. Yet, that's what is happening Sunday after Sunday in many churches. There are those who will read this chapter and learn for the first time how to become a child of God by being born into God's family through the new birth. You may be one of those. If so, it is imperative that you receive Christ now.

How Can I Be Born Again?

As Nicodemus came to Jesus that night so many years ago, we all must come to Him to receive the forgiveness He alone can give. To be born again, each of us must have a personal experience with Jesus Christ, God's Son. Has there ever been a time when you, by your own choice, invited the Lord Jesus into your life? Have you received Him? It's a choice you and you alone can make. God offers forgiveness and eternal life to those who receive His Son. Jesus alone can save you—not the church, not your good works, only Jesus. Have you had a personal experience of conversion to Jesus

Christ? Jesus said, ". . . Except ye be converted, and become as little children, ye shall not enter into the kingdom of heaven" (Matthew 18:3 KJV). Have you experienced conversion? Without conversion there is no new birth and no salvation. The words *convert* and *repent* are the same word in the New Testament. To repent means to change your mind; it means to turn around, to have a change of attitude. One who is born again is one who has changed his mind about sin and has turned himself over to Jesus Christ. Such repentance demands an act of your will. You and I must choose to turn from our sins and once and for all turn to Jesus, the Christ.

The Elements of Repentance

Here's where many church members have been confused. Some have never repented of their sins. Jesus said, ". . . except ye repent, ye shall all likewise perish" (Luke 13:3 KJV). I am convinced many would like to be converted, if only they knew how. There are three elements in repentance. Let me explain these as simply as possible.

First, you must come to hate your sin because of what it cost God to forgive it. Your sins and mine nailed Jesus to a cross. Sin is so terrible that Jesus had to die for it. When you have come to hate your sin, you must admit to God that you are a sinner. Confess your sin to God. To *confess* simply means "to agree with," "to say the same thing" about sin that God says about it. Then, believing that God has forgiven you by giving Jesus to die in your place, you must be willing to quit your life of sin and turn in faith to Jesus. You can't repent of your sin without God's help, but His Spirit will help you. All He asks is that you be willing to trust Him. When you desire a new life, He then comes to do the converting and the changing that you seek. Only Jesus Christ can give this new life.

A Life-Changing Prayer

The moment you, in prayer, cry out to the Father: "God, I am a sinner. I don't deserve Your love. Forgive my sin for Jesus' sake. I willingly turn from my sin right now. Come into my life, Lord Jesus, and save me. I receive You now as my Saviour and Lord," at that moment a miracle awaits you. Jesus Christ Himself, in the form and person of the Holy Spirit, comes to live in your spirit. In an instant you are born again. A spiritual rebirth takes place in your soul. In an instant you become a new creation in Christ (2 Corinthians 5:17). Immediately you are adopted into God's forever family (Romans 8:15).

Someone has said: You may join a temperance society and become reformed, you may join a literary society and become informed, you may join a secret society and become uniformed, you may join society and become deformed, but if you are joined to Christ, you become transformed. Praise God, let Jesus come into your life. Do it now if you haven't already done this. You must be born again!

Source Notes
1. Charles Colson, *Born Again* (Old Tappan, NJ: Fleming H. Revell, 1976). Billy Graham, *How to Be Born Again* (Waco, TX: Word Books, 1977).

Additional Reading
Colson, Charles. *Born Again*. Old Tappan, NJ: Fleming H. Revell, 1976.

Graham, Billy. *How to Be Born Again*. Waco, TX: Word Books, 1977.

Lee, Robert G. *The Must of the Second Birth*. Old Tappan, NJ: Fleming H. Revell, 1959, pp. 52–75.

Lindsey, Hal. *The Liberation of Planet Earth*. Grand Rapids, MI: Zondervan, 1974, pp. 193–201.

4 Can a Christian Lose His Salvation?

Every Christian has doubted his eternal salvation in Christ. I know I have. There have been those dark times in my life when Ole Mr. Doubt, like a thief in the night, came to rob my heart of the assurance of salvation. Mr. Doubt has attacked my faith from several fronts. I have doubted myself; because of habitual or grievous sin I have thought surely a Christian could not behave the way I behaved, and I thought I must have lost my salvation. I have doubted Christ from time to time; my faith, when weak, has questioned the deity of Jesus, His power to save, and His resurrection. Upon occasion, I have doubted the absolute authority of the Holy Bible as God's Word to me. Even as I admit these doubts, I'm sure you have also walked this road. Can a Christian really lose his salvation? Can we "fall from grace," as the saying goes? Is it possible to be saved eternally and then lose that precious gift forever?

Cultural or Scriptural?

Historically, Christians have offered differing answers to this question. Especially since the Protestant Reformation and the fracturing of the Body of Christ into denominations, there has been controversy over the "security" issue. By *security,* I mean the believer's eternal security in Christ. The issue has to do with at least two or three doctrinal perspectives. Once we affirm our freedom to interpret Scripture according to our own spiritual understanding, we open ourselves up to variant interpretations of Scripture. This is always a problem. When Scripture is interpreted different ways by different groups, it then becomes a toss-up as to who is correct. It then becomes nearly impossible to say what is culturally conditioned and what is scripturally revealed. As we shall see in a moment, there are passages in the New Testament that seem to indicate "falling from grace." How one views these passages will determine his assurance of salvation or his lack of it. Wise biblical interpretation is critical to any understanding of truth.

The Real Issue
However, the answer to this question of eternal destiny is much more than just doctrinal; it's very personal! My soul and peace of mind are at stake! And so are yours! Sometimes theologians forget the genuine soul agony people go through, seeking to find real peace with God. This being the case, we'll seek to approach this subject as practically as possible and still touch all the bases.

It seems to me that the answer to this question, "Can I lose my salvation?" is found in the answer to a prior question. That is, "How did I secure my salvation in the first place?" Does forgiveness come to me because of something I did, or was forgiveness the result of what Christ Jesus did for me? Is being saved a result of my efforts or His? Is salvation by grace or by works or a combination of both? How I answer these questions will settle the issue of whether or not I believe I can lose my salvation.

I HAD IT, BUT I LOST IT. For some, the issue is settled. Many major denominations teach falling from grace. This idea was developed by a seventeenth-century professor of theology named James Arminius. A Bible professor at the University of Leiden, he became known as the founder of Arminian theology. Among his teachings was the idea that a Christian could lose his salvation through prolonged disobedience. Today such Protestant groups as Methodists, Assembly of God, Church of Christ, the Christian Church, Freewill Baptists, and the Church of the Nazarene all are Arminian in their teaching.[1] These and others are like a man I talked to recently who said, "I used to be a Christian; I had it once, but I lost it." James Arminius was no dummy when it came to debating

Scripture; neither was John Wesley, who followed his teaching. If these men felt the Scripture taught falling from grace, they did so for what they thought were biblical reasons.

I'VE GOT IT, AND I CAN'T LOSE IT. John Calvin was a contemporary of Arminius who taught just the opposite. Calvinism embodies the concept of the eternal security of the believer. Such Protestant groups as Presbyterians, Baptists, Evangelical Free, and many independent groups have taught once saved always saved. Well, who is right?

Before I answer that question, let's look at those passages in Scripture which seem to offer the possibility of losing your eternal salvation.

> I am the vine, you are the branches; he who abides in Me, and I in him, he bears much fruit; for apart from Me you can do nothing. If anyone does not abide in Me, he is thrown away as a branch, and dries up; and they gather them, and cast them into the fire, and they are burned.
>
> John 15:5, 6

> You have been severed from Christ, you who are seeking to be justified by law; you have fallen from grace.
>
> Galatians 5:4

> So then, my beloved, just as you have always obeyed, not as in my presence only, but now much more in my absence, work out your salvation with fear and trembling.
>
> Philippians 2:12

> For in the case of those who have once been enlightened and have tasted of the heavenly gift and have been made partakers of the Holy Spirit, and have tasted the good word of God and the powers of the age to come, and then have fallen away, it is impossible to renew them again to repentance, since they again crucify to themselves the Son of God, and put Him to open shame.
>
> Hebrews 6:4–6

> For if we go on sinning willfully after receiving the

knowledge of the truth, there no longer remains a sacrifice for sins, but a certain terrifying expectation of judgment, and the fury of a fire which will consume the adversaries.

Hebrews 10:26, 27

My brethren, if any among you strays from the truth, and one turns him back, let him know that he who turns a sinner from the error of his way will save his soul from death, and will cover a multitude of sins.

James 5:19, 20

For if after they have escaped the defilements of the world by the knowledge of the Lord and Savior Jesus Christ, they are again entangled in them and are overcome, the last state has become worse for them than the first. For it would be better for them not to have known the way of righteousness, than having known it, to turn away from the holy commandment delivered to them. It has happened to them according to the true proverb, "A dog returns to its own vomit." and, "A sow, after washing, returns to wallowing in the mire."

2 Peter 2:20–22

He who overcomes shall thus be clothed in white garments; and I will not erase his name from the book of life . . . .

Revelation 3:5

That's All There Is

The above-mentioned sections of Scripture comprise the fly in the ointment of New Testament teaching that has led some to believe that a Christian can actually lose salvation. Indeed, anyone's first impression is to read these verses and agree that they do teach falling from grace. In fact, it is my understanding that one or two of these passages may teach the possibility of apostasy; but they also may not teach apostasy. The issue is certainly open to further study as we shall see. Our approach will be to decide first why man needs to be saved, and then how God has provided salvation. Then, finally, do these verses allow the possibility of losing salvation once we have received it?

A PARADOX. To begin with, to speak of being saved and then not being saved is antithetical language. It's like saying you were almost saved from being shot or almost saved from getting run over by a truck! Either you were or you weren't. If you got shot, you weren't saved from being shot. If the truck ran over you, even just part of you, you weren't saved from being squished by the truck! If language means anything, when Jesus said He came to "seek and to save" us, surely He meant what He said. Sort of saved, or temporarily saved is not very saved.

ETERNAL OR TEMPORARY? Take the word *eternal* in Scripture. It means "from age to age." It describes a forever experience. The salvation Jesus gives offers the gift of eternal life (John 3:16; John 3:36; Romans 6:23; Hebrews 7:25; 1 John 5:11–13). Obviously, if this life Jesus gives us as a gift is eternal, it can't be temporary. Jesus said, "and I give eternal life to them, and they shall never perish; and no one shall snatch them out of My hand" (John 10:28). Notice our Lord's choice of two strong words: *eternal* and *never*. If something eternal lasts forever, it makes you wonder how you can lose this forever forgiveness. If you can never perish, how can you ever perish?

GIFTS AND WAGES. Scripture speaks continually of salvation being a gift which our heavenly Father gives us. This gift is contrasted with wages. ". . . the *wages* of sin is death, but the *free gift* of God is eternal life in Christ Jesus our Lord" (Romans 6:23, *italics added*). A wage is earned; a gift is offered freely. Therefore, if salvation is not earned by something you did, how can it be lost as a result of something you do? The gift was offered by God's grace, not on the basis of man's goodness. Salvation does not begin in the merit of man, but in the mercy of God. It does not begin in the life of man, but in the home of God. It is not an attainment, but an obtainment. It is a gift, not a goal.

Amazing Grace

Receiving God's grace gift of salvation produces forgiveness and eternal life. Whether or not we can lose this gift, we must let Scripture decide. How we decide will be determined by your understanding of the concept of salvation by grace. Paul declared in Ephesians 2:8, ". . . by grace you have been saved . . . ." Let's take a moment to examine the meaning of grace salvation and all that it implies. Modern man, like his ancestors, faces a two-fold liability in the presence of Holy God:

- We are sinners by birth—sons of Adam born in sin (Romans 5:12, 19). Therefore, our very nature is sinful, self-centered, and cannot please God (Romans 8:8).
- We are sinners by choice (Romans 3:23). Therefore, we are guilty of transgressing God's moral laws.

The above two facts constitute walls, or barriers, that exist between man and God. Because of these barriers, we need two things:

- *Deliverance* from what we are—self
- *Forgiveness* for what we've done—sin

God's provision for salvation was to tear down the barriers that existed. He did something for us which we could not do for ourselves. This is critical to our understanding of how God forgives sins. Man erected the walls, or barriers, but is powerless to remove them. Man cannot change what he is inside—sinner—nor can he remove the guilt of what he has done—sinned. Man deserves justice, but he needs mercy. God's grace is that mercy. The Amplified Bible translates *grace* as "unmerited favor." It is God's love, or favor, toward us when we do not merit or earn it. Someone defined grace as:

G–God's
R–Riches
A–At
C–Christ's
E–Expense

God's grace toward us is the cross of His Son, Jesus. ". . . While we were yet sinners, Christ died for us" (Romans 5:8). That's the grace of God. Now the important thing here is that we really see what God's grace has done for us.

Four Picture Words

The New Testament writers use several picture words which illustrate what Jesus' death on the cross has done to tear down the barriers between us and Holy God.[2] I want us briefly to look at these word pictures; then we'll decide if we can lose the salvation grace bought us.

JUSTIFIED. Romans 3:24 says, "being justified as a gift by His grace through the redemption which is in Christ Jesus." Paul's first word picture is *justification,* or *justified.* This is a lawyer's term. It has great legal ramifications. Here the sinner is pictured as standing before a judge in a courtroom. All the evidence is in, and he is guilty before the great Judge of the universe: the Lord God. God as holy, righteous Judge must defend this law. The sinner is the lawbreaker, and such transgression must be punished.

The word *justified* means to declare "innocent," "not guilty" or "righteous." Paul says that is what God, the righteous Judge of the universe, has done for us. He has declared us not guilty. How did He accomplish such a feat? It wasn't easy. God was faced with a delicate dilemma. As a Holy God, He must punish sin. As a God of love, He desires to forgive the sinners. He hates sin and loves the sinner. How can He vindicate His holiness and still love the sinner? Justification was God's answer.

An act of grace. Perhaps an illustration of how God justified us would help demonstrate what the cross of Jesus did for us. Suppose I am your father. I am also a district judge. You are my rebellious teenage daughter or son. You steal an automobile, and, while driving under the influence of alcohol, you run over and kill an innocent child. By chance you are brought into my court for sentencing. All the evidence is in, and you are found guilty on several counts of lawlessness. It is my task, as judge, to pass sentence upon you—my own child. For the sake of the illustration, let's say the sentence is capital punishment—a life for a life. What a dilemma! As your loving father I desire to forgive and extend mercy, but as a judge I must honor the law and punish the lawbreaker. What is the solution? Suppose, as the judge, I came down off the judge's seat, stood beside you, and passed sentence upon myself as your substitute. My life for yours. The law would be satisfied, and you would be justified. You would be declared righteous, innocent. I would have taken your place and punishment—the innocent for the guilty. Someone said justified means, "just as if I'd never sinned." What a wonderful act of love that would be. Amazingly, that's what God, the righteous Judge, did for us. Jesus (God in the flesh [John 1:14, 18; Hebrews 1:3]) died in our place. Romans 5:8 declares, ". . . Christ died for us." God now sees the sinner just as if he'd never sinned—or *justified*. We are pardoned by the Judge of the universe.

Notice that God has declared us righteous. It is an act of His love. He sees us as innocent when He knows we are not! Jesus' righteousness has been deposited to our bankrupt account, and God sees us in Christ. We are pardoned without any merit in us. We had nothing to do with it. It is pure grace. We are acquitted, pronounced innocent, and all because of the death of Jesus, our Saviour. That's one look at how God removed the barriers. He justified us in Christ. We have been eternally pardoned, not just paroled.

REDEEMED. Jesus has also *redeemed* us, as well as pardoned us. Romans 3:24 also says, "being justified as a gift by His grace *through the redemption which is in Christ Jesus*" (*italics added*). Paul's second word picture to illustrate grace salvation through the cross is *redemption*. Even as *justification* pictures the courtroom, *redemption* pictures the slave market. It portrays the sinner as a slave to sin and the devil. Christ came to pay the ransom for our freedom. Jesus Himself used this word picture when He said, "For even the Son of Man did not come to be served, but to serve, and to give His life a ransom for many" (Mark 10:45). The Greek word for *ransom* means "the price paid to a slave owner to purchase a slave." The price that purchased us out of slavery was the precious blood of Jesus, God's dear Son. This is Simon Peter's thought when he writes, "knowing that you were not redeemed [Greek: *ransomed*] with perishable things like silver or gold from your futile way of life inherited from your forefathers, but with precious blood, as of a lamb unblemished and spotless, the blood of Christ'' (1 Peter 1:18, 19). Redemption has been purchased for us. Our freedom from sin's bondage has been paid for by the blood of Christ. We have been declared not guilty before the Law of God and also set free from slavery. We are never to be put on sale again, because we are no longer slaves, but sons, adopted into the family of God (Romans 8:15). We have been forever acquitted and emancipated! The Bible tells us at least five things about our redemption:

- It cost God the life of His only Son (1 Peter 1:18, 19).
- It has taken place, historically, on the cross (Ephesians 1:7).
- It is eternal, not temporary (Hebrews 9:12).
- It is offered to the whole world (1 Timothy 2:3–6).
- It must be appropriated by faith in the work of Jesus on the cross (Romans 3:26, 28).

PROPITIATION. Third, God's saving grace is pictured as a *propitiation* for sins. Romans 3:25 contains Paul's third graphic illustration of salvation: ''whom God displayed publicly as a propitiation in His blood through faith . . . .'' This word pictures an altar of animal sacrifice. It portrays Yom Kippur—the day of atonement, when the Jewish high priest would offer up an unblemished lamb as a sacrifice for the sins of the people. In reality, the Passover in Egypt, many centuries ago, was a foreshadowing of the cross of Jesus (1 Corinthians 5:7). *Propitiation* literally means, ''to turn away wrath by the offering of a sacrifice.'' In other words, it describes how God, through Jesus' death, cleanses the sinner and removes all guilt from him.

In Romans 5:9 we are told that we are saved from wrath through Christ. The word *wrath* means God's continuing attitude toward the flesh, or self life, in us. It is not a momentary anger, but a constant attitude of God toward the self life in us. Wrath is God's one disposition toward the sin nature in man.

Proof of God's love. What can turn away the wrath of God? Only propitiation can forever stay His wrath. Just as in Egypt God's wrath came down upon the Egyptians who opposed Moses and the Israelite slaves, even so, without propitiation, all men are under the wrath of God. In Egypt, on that first Passover, the Jews put the blood of a lamb above the door of each household, and the death angel passed them by. Blood had been offered in faith. First Corinthians 5:7 says, ". . . For Christ our Passover also has been sacrificed." When we were helplessly defiled and guilty before Holy God, He sent His Son to become the ". . . Lamb of God who takes away the sin of the world" (John 1:29). Christ has taken on Himself the full fury of the wrath of God against sin. This wrath is what made Jesus pray in the Garden of Gethsemane, ". . . let this cup pass from Me . . . ." Do you doubt God loves you? Do you question His loving care? When God knew the horrible truth about you—your vile, selfish heart—He still cared enough to put all His anger on Jesus—for you. First John 4:10 tells us that propitiation is God's greatest proof of His love for us: "In this is love, not that we loved God, but that He loved us and sent His Son to be the propitiation for our sins." Now, what are the results of Christ's sacrifice for us? What does propitiation mean to us?

First of all, God has *forever* cleansed us of all unrighteousness. His sacrifice has eternally blotted out our sins (Colossians 2:14 uses this imagery of Christ having blotted out sins. The verb tense in the original carries the idea that it is forever removed). Hebrews 7:27 tells us that Jesus, as our high priest, offers the sacrifice of Himself only once. This one sacrifice for sins removes all guilt for all times.

> For it was fitting that we should have such a high priest, holy, innocent, undefiled, separated from sinners and exalted above the heavens; who does not need daily, like those high priests, to offer up sacrifices, first for His own sins, and then for the sins of the people, because this He did *once for all* when He offered up Himself.
>
> Hebrews 7:26, 27, *italics added*

Second, this means God isn't mad at us anymore! His wrath is gone. Jesus took it for us. Therefore, when a Christian sins, he need never fear the wrath of God.[3] Through the cleansing blood of Jesus,

God has set Himself free to love us. His love is unconditional. It is grace love, unmerited favor. Even God's discipline to sinning believers is not punishment to get even for offended justice, but it is the work of love to teach us to walk by faith. Propitiation says, "God has cleansed me and loves me eternally."

RECONCILIATION. In Romans 5:10, 11, Paul uses another picture word several times. It is the family word *reconciliation*. This term is illustrated for us by our Lord Jesus, in the parable of the prodigal son (Luke 15:11–32). When the wayward son came home to his father, and the two embraced after the son's confession, that was a picture of reconciliation. To be reconciled to God basically means to be restored to fellowship with our heavenly Father, because all the barriers are down. Because the sin, guilt, and wrath are gone, we now have eternal peace with God. God is our Father; we are His children, and fellowship is secured.

Putting the Puzzle Together

Paul has been painting a picture for us. It is entitled *Saved by Grace*. This picture is like a giant puzzle. As we put the pieces together, we gain a perspective of the whole. Notice this progression:

Propitiation: God has cleansed us and removed all guilt.
Justification: God has pronounced us innocent; we are pardoned.
Redemption: God has freed us from defeat and death.
Reconciliation: As a result, we are reconciled to God and restored to fellowship.

Paul says in Colossians 1:22, "yet He has now reconciled you in His fleshly body through death, in order to present you before Him holy and blameless and beyond reproach." These are the results of grace salvation. We have forgiveness, freedom, and cleansing, so He can present us before Him ". . . holy and . . . beyond reproach." All of this simply means that God has accepted us in Christ. Sins are no longer the issue. All the barriers are gone, removed forever. No matter how many sins you've committed, nothing can keep you from God. His grace is greater than all our sin.

Confess and Receive

Because we have already been justified and already have peace with God, we are not to beg and plead for forgiveness. To do so is to call God a liar. He has already forgiven, freed, cleansed, and loved us. Well, what then is real confession of sin, if it isn't asking for forgiveness? The Greek word *confess* means to "speak the same thing." It means to "agree with." Confession means I am to agree with God about my sins. I am to say the same thing God does about them. God says they are nailed to the cross, blotted out forever—the sins I'll commit tomorrow, next year, or whenever—they were removed before I was born! When a Christian confesses his sin, he is to say, "Thank You, Jesus, for loving me and dying for me. Thank You for showing me my wrongdoing. I agree with You. This is wrong. Thank You for forgiving me, and now, by Your grace, I will go out and live as a child of God should live."

Just remember, Christian, when Satan comes to you to put his false guilt on you or to accuse you of being lost and make you feel unworthy of God's love, that you are saved by grace eternally. The barriers are removed. So when Satan comes to prosecute you before the throne of God, remember you have two counsels for your defense. Jesus is your advocate (lawyer) at the throne (1 John 2:1), and the Holy Spirit is your advocate within your heart (Colossians 3:15), and if that isn't enough to assure you, the Judge on the throne just happens to be Your Father. Amen! If God be for you, who can be against you?

Conditional Love

Anyone who has studied psychology has discovered some very interesting things about a person reared in a home where he was never sure of his parents' love. As a child, the person was given a sense of acceptance only if he performed according to the parents' standards. If the child failed, there was no sense of acceptance and self-worth. As a result, such a child will grow up desperately insecure in every relationship. Thus, he often wears a mask, pretends, and is never real, because he feels that no one could possibly like his real self. Such a person always pretends to be something he is not, in order to gain the acceptance of others. This distorted insecurity is the result of conditional love.

This can also be true in your relationship to God. Often we have the idea that God's love for us is conditional. If I do well, He then accepts me; but if I fail, then I am not accepted. This type of theology will destroy any hope of security and sense of well-being with God. If you and I do not know that God loves us regardless of our performance, then our Christian lives are going to be ones of insecurity and inconsistency. We will never learn to walk by faith, but, rather, we'll always be trying to earn God's approval or else rebelling in order to escape His disapproval.

People who have only known conditional love have great difficulty understanding the grace of God. His love is not on a performance basis. God doesn't grade on the curve. Conditional human love says to the child, "Go wash your face, and Mommy will love you." God's unmerited love toward us says, "I love you; now go wash your face." He accepts us when we are good; He accepts us when we are not good. Why? Because of our union with Christ Jesus. God chooses to deal with us, not on the basis of our sins, but rather on the basis of the merits of Christ. This is why grace salvation allows no room for losing salvation.

God Isn't an Indian Giver

What grace gives, grace does not retract. When you are born again, you cannot be unborn. There are no strings attached to God's free gift of salvation. All He asks is that we live by faith. Faith means:

> F–Forsaking
> A–All
> I–I
> T–Trust
> H–Him

Whether your faith is strong or weak, it cannot affect your acceptance with God:

Let me stress it again: salvation is all one piece. All salvation, past, present, and future, has one *base*. That base is not our faith. If we are confused here, we are confused completely. A man can never be justified on the basis of his own faith. Through all of salvation the only base is the finished work of Jesus Christ on the cross in history. Faith is the empty hand, the *instrument* by which we accept God's free gift. Faith is simply believing God. It is not a leap in the dark. It is ceasing to call God a liar, and believing Him. Justification is only on the basis of the finished work of Christ. Faith is the instrument by which we accept that finished work. This is the how, but this "how" extends through all salvation.

Consider, for example, assurance. The Bible makes it plain that the man who is a Christian has a right to know that he is saved: it is one of the good gifts of God, to know truly that he is a Christian. This refers not only to the initial fact, after one has accepted Christ as Savior, but also applies in those great and crushing moments in our lives when the waves get so high that it seems, psychologically or spiritually, that we can never find our footing again. At such a moment a Christian can have assurance. His salvation rests on the finished work of Christ, whether he accepts the peace he should have, or not; and he can have assurance *to the extent to which he believes the promises of God* at that moment.[4]

What About Those Verses?

Having established such a strong case for our security in Christ, it's now time to examine those verses that appear to say a Christian can lose his salvation. Admittedly, I approach these verses from a bias; I'm very secure in God's love and grace. However, I will seek to be as open and objective as possible.

JOHN 15:5, 6. These verses are a part of Jesus' illustration of the vine and the branches. His statement "If anyone does not abide in Me, he is thrown away as a branch, and dries up; and they gather

them, and cast them into the fire, and they are burned" has bothered
many people who see this as a declaration of being saved and then
lost. If that is our Lord's meaning, we indeed ought to be bothered!

In response to this passage, it is helpful to remember a few important principles. First, this passage is allegorical and symbolic in
language. It is always risky to build critical theology on parabolic
passages. Second, the point Jesus wants to make here is that every
Christian is to bring forth fruit for God. This is our goal in life, that
the Father be glorified by our fruit (15:8). How are we to accomplish
fruitful living that glorifies God? by abiding in Christ. Only as we are
joined to Him as a branch is to a vine can we hope to bear fruit. The
key phrase is in verse five, ". . . for apart from Me you can do
nothing." Only as Christ's life flows through us as the life of the vine
flows through the branch, can we live a Christ-like life. We are
worthless for spiritual productivity without Christ in us. This is our
Lord's point. The issue is not sin, disobedience, or rebellion that
causes us to lose salvation. The issue is fruit and abiding. He who
abides in Christ (*abiding* means "an attitude of continual dependence") will bear fruit. He who does not is spiritually worthless; that
is our Lord's meaning.

GALATIANS 5:4. This verse has the troublesome expression "falling
from grace." It reads, "You have been severed from Christ, you
who are seeking to be justified by law; you have fallen from grace."
However, this verse is the least likely to affirm that a Christian can
sin away salvation. We must read Galatians. The background of
Paul's letter is revealing. A group of Jewish Christians from
Jerusalem came to Galatia. Known as Judaizers, they followed
Paul's ministry and sought to subvert his teaching of pure grace-
plus-nothing salvation. The goal of these Judaizers was to get Gentile believers to practice Jewish traditions as a part of their commitment to Christ. For example, they demanded that the male church
members be circumcised. They insisted that Jewish feast days also
be observed. Paul's reaction was violent! He said, "I am amazed
that you are so quickly deserting Him who called you by the grace of
Christ, for a different gospel; which is really not another; only there

are some who are disturbing you, and want to distort the gospel of Christ . . . . let him be accursed" (Galatians 1:6, 7, 9).

A different gospel. Paul called this Judaizer teaching "a different gospel." He said it was a distortion of the true Gospel of grace. What was so wrong with their teaching? They were seeking to mix law and grace. They were adding to the grace of the cross of Jesus. They said forgiveness of sins comes through grace plus works. This is what angered the great apostle. In chapter two he said, ". . . knowing that a man is not justified by the works of the Law but through faith in Christ Jesus, even we have believed in Christ Jesus, that we may be justified by faith in Christ, and not by the works of the Law . . ." (v. 16). He then challenged the Galatian believers by saying, "Are you so foolish? Having begun by the Spirit, are you now being perfected by the flesh?" (Galatians 3:3.)

Sins are not the issue. Now, with this background, it is very clear that the issue is not wickedness or gross sin that causes a believer to lose salvation. The issue is how a believer is perfected after salvation. Therefore, Galatians 5:4 has absolutely nothing to do with losing salvation. Read it again in context. The first three verses deal with circumcision. Paul says that if you allow such a demand to be made upon you, you must then be obligated to keep all the Jewish laws (all 613 of them!). Second, "You have been severed from Christ, you who are seeking to be justified by law; you have fallen from grace." Therefore, falling from grace means accepting a different avenue of salvation. It means to put something in place of the cross of Jesus. The apostle never intended this phrase to imply losing salvation as a result of sins or gross disobedience. In this case, just the opposite was true. They were substituting good works for faith in Christ, and had fallen away from the principle of grace salvation. Their danger was not in giving up heaven, but in giving up their freedom.

HEBREWS 6:4–6. This paragraph in Hebrews 6 is a striking statement about "falling away" from the faith. There are those who feel these verses definitely declare that a born-again believer can lose his salvation. Before we consider what these verses mean, it is best to set the stage for the writer's words. Hebrews 6:1–9 must be read in connection with Hebrews 5:12–14. There are no chapter divisions in the original text, and this division here is unfortunate. Hebrews 5:12–14 is addressed to believers who ought to be mature in their faith, but instead they are babes. They are only ready for the ABCs of the faith. Hebrews 6 begins with a *therefore;* it says, "Therefore leave the ABC's and go on to maturity." The writer then lists six doctrines which are foundation stones of the house of faith:

- Repentance
- Faith
- Baptism
- Laying on of hands
- Resurrection of Christ
- Eternal judgment

The writer's point is that it is time for these believers to grow up, to ". . . press on to maturity . . ." (6:1). He then warns them of the danger of holding back and refusing to grow. He says, "If you should fall away, it is impossible to renew you again to repentance" (*see* Hebrews 6:6).

Who are these people? Now, the real question is: Are these people real Christians or just pretenders? How you answer determines your understanding of these words: "If they shall fall away" (Hebrews 6:6 KJV).

Dr. C. I. Scofield, editor of the famous Scofield Bible, says these people are not Jewish Christians, but rather Jews in the Jewish church; they were not real born again believers.[5] They just came in to investigate Christianity; but, due to persecution by fellow Jews, they were considering going back to Judaism. This answer is an easy out for those who do not want to deal with the problem of apostasy.[6] However, even though I personally do not believe these verses teach apostasy, I cannot agree with C. I. Scofield. This interpretation that verses four through six refer to a lost church member raises at least three problems:

- It would mean a lost church member could never become a saved church member. Verse six would be made to say it is impossible for them to repent and be saved. We know this is not true.
- Such an interpretation would mean that the unpardonable sin is to become a lost church member. I happen to know multitudes of lost church members who have been saved. I was one of them myself!
- The language of verses four and five does not describe a lost person. The writer gives us a five-fold description of these people:

1. They have been enlightened.
2. They have tasted the heavenly gift.
3. They are partakers of the Holy Spirit.
4. They have tasted the good Word of God.
5. They have experienced the power of the Lord in their lives.

Scofield and others have explained that these lost Jewish church members were *enlightened,* but did not really *see* the light of the Gospel. They *tasted,* but did not *eat* the heavenly gift and the Word of God. They *went along with* the Holy Spirit, but did not *receive* the Holy Spirit. They were lost.

Can this explanation be defended with a serious word study? I do not think so. The language and word pictures are very strong here. It's as though the writer of Hebrews 6 went to great ends to describe exactly who he was referring to. The words *once enlightened* literally mean "to shed light upon." In Ephesians 1:18 and Hebrews 10:32 this is used to describe a Christian. The word *tasted* used here means to "eat, to partake of, to enjoy." The word is used of Jesus *tasting* death for us in Hebrews 2:9. Jesus experienced death for us; He partook of death for us. He didn't just "tongue taste" it, He "gobbled it up" for us. I can see no sense in which this word can mean a lost person tastes of the heavenly gift of salvation. Such a rendering denies the sense of the word. First Peter 2:3 (NEB) says "Surely you have tasted that the Lord is good." *Tasted,* here, means "experienced." In Hebrews 6 we are told these people tasted God's

Word, and it tasted good to them. Can this be said of an unbeliever, even a religious unbeliever? The strongest argument against this interpretation is the phrase in verse four, ". . . made partakers of the Holy Spirit." This word *partaker* means to "share in, participate in, or to belong to." [7] It is used five times by Paul in 1 Corinthians. All five references describe a believer sharing in Christ's life. In Hebrews 3:1 we read, ". . . holy brethren, partakers of a heavenly calling . . . ." Again in 3:14 he writes, "For we have become partakers of Christ . . . ." Thus, this word is used to depict a believer's sharing in something of God each time. Now, in this phrase these people partake of the Holy Spirit. In what sense can a lost person share in the Holy Spirit? none whatsoever.[8] Only a born-again child of God partakes of the Holy Spirit (Jude 19; Romans 8:9). The final word on this is from Hebrews itself. In Hebrews 12:9, 10, this word is used twice, both times to affirm our salvation.

Lost or saved? What conclusion must we draw from these word studies? It seems clear to me that the writer was very careful to describe these people who need to ". . . press on to maturity." They have been made to see; they experienced the gift of God and began to share life in the Spirit. They started growing in the Word and even tasted the power of God in their lives. These are those of whom he spoke in 5:12–14. They were saved and on the way to maturity. Then they held back. They were saved, but hindered. Does this then mean they, as believers, have fallen away and lost their salvation? Not necessarily.

A paraphrase. It might be helpful now to paraphrase Hebrews 6:4–6. "If a Christian should turn aside [a literal translation of *fall away*] from the faith, it is impossible for him to repent and turn back to the faith, because Jesus would have to be crucified all over again."

Saved and resaved. Assuming this is the correct interpretation of this passage, then what does it say about those believers who refuse to grow and turn aside from Christ to something else? To me it says very directly that *if* they can turn away, they cannot turn back. *If* they can be saved then lost, then they cannot be resaved.

Now, whatever Hebrews 6 says, it at least says that much. Those who believe a Christian can lose his salvation need to really face this fact. If you take this position, then Hebrews 6:6 says you cannot be saved, lost, repent, and be resaved, which is what nearly all who believe in falling from grace practice. All of the falling-from-grace groups I know anything about, say you can lose salvation through gross sin and then repent and regain salvation. So, if Hebrews 6 teaches falling away, it also teaches permanent apostasy. If you had it and lost it, you've had it!

A hypothetical case. There is a third and more probable interpretation of these verses. Dr. Kenneth Wuest, in his *Word Studies of the New Testament,* calls verse six a hypothetical phrase. He notes that the phrase, "If they shall fall away . . ." is only one word in Greek. It is a participle. Wuest describes the participle as a conditional participle, setting up a hypothetical if–then situation. The meaning would then be this: "If it were possible for a true Christian to fall away from Jesus and turn to something else for salvation, it then would be impossible to save him again, because he rejected the New Testament sacrifice of the cross.[9] That sacrifice was once and for all, never to be repeated. So they could never be resaved." Dr. Wuest says no real Christian would ever turn away like that, therefore, the writer of Hebrews is telling them that if they fall away, it is proof that they were not saved in the first place.

I think this is the truth of Hebrews 5:12–6:6. He is saying that no real believer would ever turn away from Jesus. Those who are thinking of doing so and then do so are proving their lostness and cutting themselves off from the only means of salvation: the cross of Christ. This interpretation is compatible with 1 John 2:19, "They went out from us, but they were not really of us; for if they had been of us, they would have remained with us; but they went out, in order that it might be shown that they all are not of us."

SECOND PETER 2:20–22. The phrase in 2 Peter 2:22, ". . . A dog returns to its own vomit" has enticed some to declare that this is a picture of the believer returning to his old life of sin. Is this what Peter means? Not at all. Again we must look at the whole epistle to get a clear understanding of these verses. We must read verse one of this chapter to see who these people are of whom Peter spoke. Peter was dealing with a group of false teachers who secretly introduced destructive heresies among believers. They also denied, ". . . the Master who bought them . . ." (2 Peter 2:1). They were lost, unsaved, false teachers. This whole chapter describes them. Peter then concluded about them, ". . . it would be better for them not to have known the way of righteousness, than having known it, to turn away from the holy commandment delivered to them" (2 Peter 2:21). So you see, these verses do not refer to a believer's losing salvation after he was saved. Here Peter was speaking of those who came right up to the door of salvation, perverted the truth, then turned back to their sensual ways.

JAMES 5:19, 20. Finally, we come to this last passage. James 5:19, 20 says, "My brethren, if any among you strays from the truth, and one turns him back; let him know that he who turns a sinner from the error of his way will save his soul from death, and will cover a multitude of sins."

This passage again has been used by some to support falling from grace. These verses in themselves could mean a number of things. The problem is the phrase, ". . . save his soul from death . . . ." What is meant by *death?* A number of alternatives have been offered:

- If a Christian strays from the truth, turn him back and save his soul from the death of hell. If this is the meaning, the verse teaches apostasy.
- If a Christian sins, turn him back and save his soul from the death of lost fellowship here on earth.
- "Save his soul" could have the idea of "delivering his personality" from death. It would thus translate, "deliver his life from the deadly results of sin." This interpretation is the most probable meaning (*see* James 4:8).

The phrase: ". . . and will cover a multitude of sins" could have two meanings:

- The person who helps the wayward brother will store up forgiveness for himself and cover a multitude of his sins.

> This is not consistent with the rest of the New Testament, which opposes works as merit for salvation.
> • The probable meaning is that the one who helps a wayward Christian turn back to the Lord keeps him from committing a multitude of sins, and thus saves him from the deadly result of what sin does.

Here again, this statement by James cannot be taken to mean a believer loses salvation when it is compared to the general teaching of Scripture regarding the security of the believer.

We have taken great pains in this chapter to discuss thoroughly this matter of assurance. Why? Because this is the foundation upon which the house of faith is built. It will influence how you feel about many other questions I shall seek to answer. I believe God the Father wants you and me to be secure in our relationship with Him. I agree with John Wesley, who, even though he did not teach eternal security, possessed it himself. He said he wanted, ". . . a faith which none could have without knowing that he hath it." I concur. We all need that kind of salvation.

Source Notes

1. Roman Catholic theology also offers no security to its adherents. The Roman Catholic Church has traditionally offered a faith-plus-works program of salvation.
2. Hal Lindsey, *The Liberation of Planet Earth* (Grand Rapids, MI: Zondervan, 1974). This book has a detailed discussion of these word pictures and grace salvation.
3. We must distinguish between God's discipline (His love) and His wrath. When we sin, we never feel His wrath, only the strength of His love calling us back to Him.
4. Francis Schaeffer, *True Spirituality* (Wheaton, IL: Tyndale House, 1971), pp. 77, 78.
5. See the Scofield Bible for notes on this passage: Hebrews 6:1–6.
6. The word *apostasy* means "to fall away from the faith." It comes from the Greek words *apo,* "away," and *stasis,* "to stand." Thus it means to "stand away" or "fall away."

7. See William E. Vine's *Expository Dictionary of New Testament Words* (Old Tappan, NJ: Fleming H. Revell) for the word *partake*, in Greek, *metoxos*.

8. C. I. Scofield, in the Scofield Bible, says this word *partake* means to "go along with." This is not correct. The Greek literally means to "have together with." *To have* and *to go along with* are not the same.

9. The King James Version uses the phrasing *if* he should fall away. The New American Standard Version omits the conditional idea by translating the verb "and then have fallen away."

Additional Reading

Lindsey, Hal. *The Liberation of Planet Earth*. Grand Rapids, MI: Zondervan, 1974.

Nee, Watchman. *The Normal Christian Life*. Fort Washington, PA: Christian Literature Crusade, 1961, chapters 1, 2.

Thomas, Ian. *The Mystery of Godliness*. Grand Rapids, MI: Zondervan, 1964, chapter 8.

Stanford, Miles. *The Principle of Position*. Box 9574, Hong Kong: Living Springs Press.

Schaeffer, Francis. *True Spirituality*. Wheaton, IL: Tyndale House, 1971.

5 *How Can I Overcome Habitual Sin?*

Many Christians have what I call hangover sin. These are habits from the old life that are carried over into the new life in Christ. Do you have hangover sin in your life? Is there some addictive or enslaving habit you'd like to quit, but can't? Often the new Christian needs help in knowing how to gain deliverance from such habits. Then, too, often the problem isn't many sins, but rather one or two besetting or habitual areas of bondage.

Born to Be Victorious
Jesus saved us to live an abundant life, a life of freedom and purpose. Bondage to a crippled and enslaved will does not honor our Saviour. The salvation Christ won for us is twofold; He has saved us from both the penalty and the power of sin. Paul says, "Let not sin therefore reign in your mortal body . . ." (Romans 6:12).

Therefore, in answer to the question "how can I overcome habitual sin?" let's begin by declaring that God has not willed our defeat. As Ethel Waters said, "God don't sponsor no flops!" There is a way of escape. You can overcome any temptation. First Corinthians 10:13 says it very plainly, "No temptation has overtaken you but such as is common to man; and God is faithful, who will not allow you to be tempted beyond what you are able, but with the temptation will provide the way of escape also, that you may be able to endure it." So let's examine God's Word to discover His way of escape from habitual sin.

59

THREE ENEMIES. Every Christian has at least three enemies. His life will not go unopposed. Daily he faces the world, the flesh, and the devil. This unholy trinity seeks to defeat his walk with God, destroy his joy, and stop his witness for Christ. A life of victory can only come when he knows who the enemy is. Continually, I meet believers who put all the blame on themselves. "I guess I'm just weak," I hear someone say. Well, that may be true, but it is not the whole truth! We are in a battle, not a cakewalk! Satan does not want us to live victoriously. The enemy should get his share of the credit for our bondage.[1]

Even the great apostle knew defeat. ". . . I am of flesh, sold into bondage to sin" (Romans 7:14). Remember, ". . . our struggle is not against flesh and blood, but against the rulers, against the powers, against the world forces of this darkness, against the spiritual forces of wickedness in the heavenly places" (Ephesians 6:12).

Satan is an enemy to be reckoned with. When you are saved, he has lost your soul for all eternity, but he often continues to destroy your happiness as a believer. A carnal, defeated Christian does much advertising for the devil, and very little for our Lord.

FAITH IN THE FACTS. Overcoming temptation begins in knowing the Adversary and in believing what God tells us about our victory. Many times the Christian is trying to fight a war that is already over, and he's losing most of the time! The Bible declares that our Lord Jesus has already defeated the enemy for us. So if you are in bondage to a sin habit, it is for one of three reasons:

- You are ignorant of the facts of Christ's victory for you.
- You lack the faith to trust in Christ's power to overcome sin in your life.
- You do not want to overcome your sin.

I believe that you want all God has for you, and I have some good news for you. Because faith comes by hearing, I want briefly to review what God's Word tells us about how to walk in victory. Then you can daily apply it to your battle plan.

THE CONDITION OF THE LOST MAN. Before Jesus came, Satan had

a legal claim on us. The wages of sin is death, and we owed the evil one wages. Our sin had made us bondslaves to the devil. Second Timothy 2:26 says the lost person is in ". . . the snare of the devil, having been held captive by him to do his will." Jesus said everyone who commits sin is a slave to sin. Second Corinthians 4:4 tells us that the god of this world has blinded the eyes of the unbelieving. So we know two things about the condition of the lost person: He is bound and blind. The devil has him lock, stock, and barrel. What a pitiful condition!

THE CONQUEST OF CHRIST. The Lord Jesus has done something wonderful about this condition. He has set the captives free! Second Corinthians 10:4, 5 describes our Lord's conquest:

> For the weapons of our warfare are not of the flesh, but divinely powerful for the destruction of fortresses. We are destroying speculations and every lofty thing raised up against the knowledge of God, and we are taking every thought captive to the obedience of Christ.

The apostle illustrates the victory of Christ over the devil by picturing a walled fortress under attack. Our Christ is attacking "fortresses" to set us free. What are those walled fortresses? He says they are speculations, every lofty thing raised us against the knowledge of God, and every thought that is against God's will. Through Christ we can tear down these walls of resistance. Paul is speaking of habitual sin habits in us that are satanic strongholds that enslave us and keep us from a life of obedience to God. He tells us that we don't have to fight these sin habits and thoughts with weapons of our own strength. We have divinely powerful weapons to tear down these strongholds. We are sons and daughters, not slaves held in bondage.

Hebrews tells us that Jesus has rendered the devil powerless: ". . . that through death He might render powerless him who had the power of death, that is, the devil" (Hebrews 2:14). The Apostle John declares that Jesus came for the very purpose of destroying the works of the devil (1 John 3:8).

An Absolute Victory

What these verses tell us is that Satan may be a roaring lion, but our Lord has pulled all his teeth out! He's just a pussycat to Jesus!

Now Jesus' victory over the devil is an absolute victory. Believe that! Here is where the Christian's victory begins. Satan is running a bluff. He's running around as a roaring lion, trying to bully folks who are ignorant of Christ's victory over him. He has no power over the child of God.

Do you allow sin habits to reign over you? Often, a Christian will tolerate habitual sin when he need not do so. This happens for several reasons. Sometimes he has little or no conscience about a sin habit. A stronghold in the believer can be a defiled conscience. You've heard it said, "Let your conscience be your guide." Watch out; that is only a half-truth. We can train our consciences to rationalize and justify almost any dastardly deed! When this is the problem, we need light from the Scriptures and the convicting work of Christ's Spirit within us to show us what He considers sin, not what we choose to call sin. Oftentimes we tolerate what we know to be sin, simply because we have such little confidence in ourselves and such little faith in God. Satan has convinced us we are defeated. He has run his bluff and won it.

I recently counseled a woman who is excessively overweight. She just could not stop eating! At times she had rationalized that she had a gland problem. However, she was now convinced it was wrong to be so overweight. Yet she was hopelessly defeated. She had no confidence God could help her. She, like Paul, cried out, "Wretched man [fat woman] that I am!" (Romans 7:24.) Well, I shared with her what I'm about to share with you. There is hope: ". . . greater is he [Jesus] that is in you, than he [the devil] that is in the world" (1 John 4:4 KJV). Our Lord's victory over sin and death is for us; it is in our behalf. We need to know how to claim His victory as our own.

An Appropriated Victory

Every Christian shares in Christ's victory over evil. His death, resurrection, and ascension to the throne were for you. We share His victory. In fact, everything that can be said of Jesus' triumph over sin can be said of the believer. We are co-heirs with Christ

(Romans 8:17). When He died, we died; when He rose, we rose; when He ascended, we ascended. Ephesians 2:6 tell us that God has ". . . seated us with Him in the heavenly places, in Christ Jesus." What that means for the Christian is that he reigns with Christ in victory. We don't have to sin! Satan and any habitual sin need not defeat us. A friend of mine has said, "You don't have to tolerate anything outside the will of God in your life." He is right. What then is the problem? *Faith is the problem!* Our victory is absolute, but it must be appropriated by faith. Do you know what victorious Christian living is? It is learning to bring Calvary's victory up-to-date in your life. It is simply, by faith, applying the cross to your situation. Any born-again child of God who truly wants to live a life of fellowship with God can do so. I have discovered that every problem in my life is due to my failure to believe God. He has made provision for us, but faith is what lays hold of that provision.

Christ in You

The Scriptures tell us two wonderful truths that make overcoming temptation possible. First, as we have learned, *we are in Christ.* We are one with Him; His victory is ours. Everything that can be said about Jesus' victory over sin can be said about us. We share His victory in potential.

Second, *Christ is in you.* The Victor lives in the victim! You, the victim have the Victor (Jesus Christ) living in you. Dr. Stephen Olford says it well: "Every demand that is made on my life is in reality a demand made upon the life of Jesus within me." Greater is He that is in me, than he that is in the world! (1 John 4:4.) The Christ who lives in me can live out His life through me. Faith is the key to allowing Christ to live through me. Faith means dependent trust in another for my needs.

Set Free

Now, how can you overcome this sin habit? If your faith really believes these truths, then put your faith to work.

Acknowledge His presence within. Because Jesus lives in you, you never face temptation alone. Christ in you wants to meet the tempter and his temptation for you. When Satan knocks at your heart's door, send Jesus to the door! Satan will flee. How do you do this? All right, you are convinced you have this sin habit, this Satanic stronghold. Your will is gone; you are weak. Satan has won out in this area of your life. First, have you genuinely confessed this sin to God? If not, do so. Tell the Father you hate this sin and desire to turn from it. Ask Him to take authority over it. Now, give the problem to the Problem Solver. Give it to Jesus, who lives within you. It is now His problem. You are out of the picture. Believe this. By faith, stand on it as true.

Assert your position in Him. Declare to the devil that you are one with Christ. Let him know you believe in your victory with Christ. Call his bluff! Here I suggest you speak out directly to the evil one. Yes, talk to the devil! I do it all the time! Now, listen, Satan is not afraid of you or me! Yet he does fear and respect our Lord Jesus! Only as you are joined to Jesus by faith will the devil listen to your commands. First John 5:4 says, ". . . and this is the victory that overcomes the world—our faith." It is a dangerous thing to go around rebuking the devil in your own strength. You'll only awaken a sleeping bear! He may really devour you for breakfast! Yet, if you believe you have the victory through Christ, then you *do* have the victory, and the devil knows it. He fears only our faith in the name of Jesus. Mark 16:17 assures us: ". . . making use of my name they shall put demons to chase . . ." (authors's translation).

- Utter the command of faith—Mark 16:17
  Now comes the moment of truth. Do you *really* want to be free? If so, ask God's forgiveness. Thank Him for the blood of Jesus that cleanses from all sin (1 John 1:7, 9). Speak your faith. Declare your freedom. In Jesus' name, speak your victory. Tell God you believe He can and has given you deliverance over this sin.
- Utter the command to be free—Matthew 18:18

Tell the devil to loose you in Jesus' name. If you truly
believe in your oneness with Christ, he must obey you.
Bring every thought captive to Christ according to 2
Corinthians 10:5. "Satan, I command you to set me free
from this sin."

• Utter the command to flee—James 4:7
Order Satan to flee from you. James 4:7 promises us he
will split! Stand upon the authority of God's Word.

Is the battle over? Not necessarily. Satan doesn't give up easily.
He'll test your faith. He'll tempt again and again. You must meet
him each time the same way. Christ Jesus is your life. He'll fight for
you. As you daily drive the enemy off the battlefield of your will,
he'll soon give up. When he knows you know he's licked, he'll go
find someone else with less knowledge and less faith. Satan has too
many folks who are easy pickin's to mess with those who put Christ
in the fight each time he tempts. Make up your mind to live in
victory, then, by faith, do warfare until you are free. Amen!

Sinless Perfection?

A final word here. Victorious Christian living is not a life of sinless
perfection. Only Jesus has accomplished that. Yet, it is a life free of
bondage to habitual sin. It is a life in which you are so close to God
that any sin committed pricks your renewed and undefiled conscience. You are sensitive to the Spirit's voice. When He shows you
sin, you immediately choose to confess it, and fellowship is restored. You are walking in the light and have fellowship with your
Saviour. It is a life where sin is a stranger to you. You will not allow
it to have a home in your heart. This is the life God has for all of us.
Claim it; walk in it! Enjoy it!

Source Notes

1. A Christian's bondage should be described as an *oppression* by
the devil—that is, an area where the believer's will is held captive. There is a strong debate as to whether or not a Christian can
be demonized. This is discussed in detail in chapter six.

Additional Reading

Basham, Don. *Deliver Us From Evil.* Lincoln, VA: Chosen Books, 1972.

Lovett, C. S. *Dealing With the Devil.* Baldwin Park, CA: Personal Christianity, 1967.

Taylor, Jack R. *Victory Over the Devil.* Nashville, TN: Broadman Press, 1973.

6 *Can a Christian Be Demon Possessed?*

A very attractive, dark-haired, dark-eyed young woman gave her life to Jesus through the ministry of a large church. During the weeks that followed, she experienced all the joys and happiness that accompany salvation. She had been truly saved, born into the family of God. Then suddenly she became depressed and suicidal. She came to me for counseling, and revealed that recently she had been bombarded by inexplicable sensual thoughts. Sexual desires seemed to possess her mind. Only the week before she had her first sexual experience with an almost total stranger. This behavior led her to attempt suicide; she became hounded by deep depression.

As we talked, through tears of confession, she sobbed, "What's happened to me? I was such a nice girl and so happy to be a Christian. How could I do what I've done, and why do these bad thoughts haunt me so?" Thinking that her first need was to be aware of God's love and forgiveness, I opened my Bible and began to read. Suddenly her body tensed, and with eyes flashing, she blurted out, "What's that?" "It's a Bible," I replied. She pushed my Bible aside and turned her head away.

Changing my approach, I put the Bible away and began to ask the girl to tell me some facts about herself: How long she had been a Christian, where she came from, and how long she had lived in the area. As she talked, a fascinating story unfolded. The girl was a full-blooded Indian. Her father was a chief in her tribe, and she and her brother were princess and prince among her people. She had been raised among all the ritual and religion of her tribe most of her life; she sat in on yearly pow-wows and heard many prayers lifted up to pagan gods.

Soon after becoming a Christian, she had gone with her family to a great gathering of her tribe. Because she had just turned eighteen, she had come of age; and part of the pow-wow centered around her as princess of the tribe. She sat for hours, surrounded by the medicine men of her tribal council. For days she sat dressed in regal Indian splendor, as the medicine men, who were the priests and religious leaders of her people, prayed their prayers over her. She was being dedicated to the gods of her Indian people.

One of the highlights of the pow-wow was an official dance by the princess. She was a debutante being initiated into tribal society. It was a great moment; she had looked forward to it for years. How proud she was! Yet horror awaited her, and had she known what the results were to be, she would never have danced that dance or submitted to the ritual of the medicine men.

Dressed in a very beautiful and sensual gown, the dance she did was to symbolize her offering herself to the gods of her tribe. In essence, it was a profession of faith, though she did not mean it to be that. She did this to please her family and her people, and she thought it would be exciting.

She danced to a number of specific gods. One dance was directed toward the war god, the god of revenge upon the historical enemies of her tribe. The main dance was to the totem of a giant Thunderbird; the purpose of the dance was to give her to him completely.[1]

Any one of us, watching that beautiful pageantry, would have been thrilled by the splendor of it all. But it is amazing how Satan can disguise himself. Little could we know what unseen forces were at work that day. The Scriptures never lie; Paul declared centuries ago:

> What do I mean then? That a thing sacrificed to idols is anything, or that an idol is anything? No, but I say that the things which the Gentiles sacrifice, *they sacrifice to demons,* and not to God; and I do not want you to become sharers in demons.
>
> 1 Corinthians 10:19, 20, italics added

This attractive teenage girl had no idea she was participating in demon worship, yet she was. Paul's words were proved true, and she had become a sharer in demons; she had opened herself to the unseen world of the demonic. The problems she had with depression, sensuality, hatred, and carnality were the result of that initiation ritual.

After hearing her story for about an hour, I explained the possibilities of demonic oppression as the result of her experiences at the pow-wow. As I and other Christian ministers began to pray for this girl's deliverance, it was revealed to us that evil spirits had entered her body, corresponding to the nature and personality of each totem god she had danced to. As a result of the dance to the war god, a demon of hate oppressed her, speaking out in a different voice from the girl's. Each time a demon was exorcised, the girl received more peace. The archdemon who had invaded her was a demon of lust, whose name was the tribal name for the Thunderbird. When we told her he had spoken to us through her and had used this name to identify herself, the girl was shocked and surprised to learn that we knew the name.

After prayer, repentance, and renouncing all ties and vows made to these demon gods, the girl was completely delivered. Her spiritual and emotional health returned, and she began to grow as a Christian. But she had learned a valuable lesson about the reality of Satan.

What are we to think? This is a provocative illustration of the way Satan can work in the lives of Christians today. Many persons who are believers in Christ are skeptical about demons and demon possession. In my work with runaway youth on Sunset Strip in Hollywood, I was forced into facing the drug culture and the occult world that accompanies it. I can assure you that the existence of demons is real, because I have faced them more than once.

This girl's experience can raise many questions:

• Was she really saved prior to going to that Indian pow-wow?
• Was she possessed by evil spirits?
• Is there another explanation for her problem, other than demons?
• What can demons do to Christians?

What Is Demon Possession?

What are we to make of all this? There are some statements regarding the Christian's relationship to demon activity which must be made. Although Satan does not need more publicity, for he certainly gets his share of it, there is little attention given to what the Christian's attitude toward the Satanic world should be.

First, let's define what demon possession means. Dr. Merrill F. Unger, in his book *Demons in the World Today,* says:

> Demon possession is a condition in which one or more evil spirits or demons inhabit the body of a human being and can take complete control of their victim at will. By temporarily blotting out his consciousness they can speak and act through him as their complete slave and tool. The inhabiting demon (or demons) comes and goes much like the proprietor of a house who may or may not be "at home." When the demon is "at home," he may precipitate an attack. In these attacks the victim passes from his normal state, in which he acts like other people, to the abnormal state of possession.[2]

This definition sounds like an exact description of the teenage girl I helped. Yet she was a Christian who seemed at times to be totally possessed by a host of evil spirits. How can this happen to a believer? I only know that missionaries often report that those who become Christians out of idol-worship backgrounds are very open to repossession, should they return to such worship.[3]

Dr. Unger notes that the term *demon possession* does not appear in the Bible.[4] The New Testament description of people in this condition is a participle which literally translates "demonized." The Bible would say Jesus encountered a demonized person. These New Testament accounts do not describe this further as being possessed, oppressed, invaded, or anything else. It simply says that a person was a demoniac, or demonized.

I have a rather extensive library on the occult and demons. One is hard put to find an author who believes that a Christian can be demon possessed. Some will allow the possibility exists that demons can *invade* a Christian's body, but they cannot *possess* him. The argument is that demons can live in the human body, but total possession would mean the evil spirit had taken over the human soul and human spirit. Now, since the Holy Spirit lives in the human spirit of a believer, a demon could not possess a Christian by living where the Holy Spirit lives. That's how the argument against a Christian being totally possessed is formulated. Those who feel this way have used terms like *invaded* or *oppressed* by demons rather than *possessed*. These terms are helpful, and I'm not critical of such distinctions.

In one sense, every human being is demonized. Satan is the god of this world, and he tempts, pressures, and suggests evil to all human flesh—Christians as well as non-Christians. Everyone has been visited by demons in one way or another. In its less severe form, demon attacks come to us from without, through temptations and pressure. As we yield to sin, the result is increased demon influence in our lives. This is just another way of saying that as we disobey repeatedly, the devil gets his hold on us; habitual sin allows the devil to put our very will in bondage.

Scripture reveals many levels of demonization. It can manifest itself in different ways. The following passages reveal demon activity in the life of apparent believers.

- Demons can cause believers to backslide (1 Timothy 4:1).
- Demons can produce doctrinal corruption (1 John 4:1).
- Demon-led doctrine influences believers toward evil conduct (1 Corinthians 10:16–22).
- Demon influence leads to loving pleasure more than God (2 Timothy 2:26–3:4).
- Demon influence leads to defiling lust (2 Peter 2:10–14).

In all these passages there is an open debate concerning whether or not the persons referred to were genuine Christians, but certainly they considered themselves believers.

Demonic influence may become so severe that it is no longer temptation from without. The evil spirits or spirit may actually come to live in the body of the person. This is true of the Christian as well as the non-Christian.

Can a Christian Be Invaded?

What scriptural evidence, if any, is there for claims that a Christian can have demons living in him? We are warned in Scripture of the danger of living in persistent sin. Paul mentions two believers, Hymenaeus and Alexander, who had gone "shipwreck" in their faith so much so that Paul had ". . . delivered [them] over to Satan, so that they may be taught not to blaspheme" (1 Timothy 1:20). As to just what the apostle meant by that phrase, ". . . delivered over to Satan . . ." I'm not sure, but I'm glad it wasn't me! Whatever it means, it doesn't sound good!

Again in 1 Corinthians 5:5, Paul is trying to decide what to do about a fellow who persisted in sex sin. He says, "I have decided to deliver such a one to Satan for the destruction of his flesh, that his spirit may be saved in the day of the Lord Jesus."

Although these verses do not teach actual demon possession, they show that the apostle felt that these brothers were so far gone that he had given up on them and saw no recourse but to let Satan do as he pleased in their lives. The results of Satan's attack may be physical or mental sickness or even death. Whether or not a Christian can be indwelt by demons is a subject that Scripture is silent about. These verses only give us a key. My experience in counseling has led me to believe that a Christian may be indwelt by demons.

Dr. Unger distinguishes between being invaded and being possessed this way: In the case of severe demon influence, the demon comes into the body as a visitor or guest, whereas in total possession they own the house. The results are different. Possession is evidenced by total personality takeover.[5]

All illustrations fail in this instance, because we are seeking to describe a spiritual reality, not a physical phenomenon. Suffice it to say, however, that a Christian becomes a house divided against itself. With God and the devil living in the same house, what conflict the soul must endure!

How does a Christian come to this degraded state in which he allows Satan residence in his life? Remember Judas Iscariot, who, although he was so close to Jesus, probably was not a true believer. How could he have missed all that Jesus had for him, to the point where ". . . Satan . . . entered into him . . ."? (John 13:27.)

Satan can enter any one of us, given the opportunity. This may happen in a variety of ways, but always someone must ". . . give place to the devil," as the Bible declares (Ephesians 4:27 KJV).

Demon possession or invasion can occur through these means:

- *Through being passed on from parents to children.* The words of Moses are true that the sins of the parents are passed down even to the third and fourth generations. Parents who are involved in witchcraft and the occult arts open their children to demonic influence.
- *Through direct occult involvement.* Anyone who dabbles in the occult world is openly inviting Satan into his life. He will accept the invitation. Such seemingly harmless activities as astrology and horoscopes increase demonic influence in one's life.
- *Through sexual immorality.* Demons have been attracted to someone by means of sexual intercourse with a witch or warlock. Sexual involvement with those deep in occult practices is an open door to the evil one.
- *Through habitual sin.* Christians and non-Christians alike can become addicted to sin habits which allow a demonic stronghold. Practicing habitual sin is a form of witchcraft, and those who do so are on the devil's side in those areas of bondage.
- *Through returning to idolatry.* As in the case of the Indian princess described earlier, those who have come from idol worship are very susceptible to being demonized, should they ever return to such practices. This is also true of former practitioners of occult arts.

Actually, whether or not a Christian can be totally possessed is only a speculative question. The real issue is that we all may be severely demonized, to the point of being given over to the evil one. We must be awake to the influences of the supernatural world, and "Abstain from all appearance of evil" (1 Thessalonians 5:22 KJV). Far too many persons are dabbling in the various aspects of the occult and are ignorant of the dangers involved. We know so little of the wiles of the evil one; he is a roaring lion seeking to devour us. May God give us grace to turn from evil, seek the good, and grow in grace and the knowledge of our Lord, Jesus Christ. The Christian's greatest resource is to be filled with the Holy Spirit. He or she who is Spirit filled has no fear of being filled with anyone or anything else.

Source Notes

1. The Thunderbird, in many Indian cultures, is the counterpart of the Great Spirit. He is the god of the earth: the god of thunder, rain, and so on. In Christian terminology, he is the god of this world. As we came to discover, the totem Thunderbird was a cover for Satan himself.
2. Merrill F. Unger, *Demons in the World Today* (Wheaton, IL: Tyndale House, 1971), p. 102.
3. Hobart E. Freeman, *Deliverance From Occult Oppression and Subjection* (Claypool, IN: Faith Publications, 1968), pp. 47, 48. *See* also A. J. MacMillan, *Modern Demon Possession* (Harrisburg, PA: Christian Pubns., Inc., 1942), pp. 3–5, 17. MacMillan gives examples of demon possession of an uninstructed believer, as the result of dabbling in spiritism.
4. Unger, *Demons,* p. 101.
5. Unger, *Demons,* p. 115.

Additional Reading

Basham, Don. *Deliver Us From Evil.* Lincoln, VA: Chosen Books, 1972.

Koch, Kurt. *Between Christ and Satan.* Grand Rapids, MI: Kregel Pubns., 1962.

Koch, Kurt. *Demonology, Past and Present.* Grand Rapids, MI: Kregal Pubns., 1973.

Koch, Kurt. *The Devil's Alphabet.* Grand Rapids, MI: Kregal Pubns., 1969.

Koch, Kurt. *Occult Bondage and Deliverance.* Stuttgart, W. Germany: Evangelization Publishers, 1970.

Needham, Mrs. George C. *Angels and Demons.* Chicago: Moody Press.

Philpott, Kent. *A Manual of Demonology and the Occult*. Grand Rapids, MI: Zondervan, 1973. This book is the most practical book available for the layman who seeks answers in this area.
Unger, Merrill F. *Demons in the World Today*. Wheaton, IL: Tyndale House, 1976.

7 Does God Want to Heal All Sickness?

There seems to be a good deal of confusion on this topic. Faith healers have confronted the American television-viewing public with their claim that God will heal everyone, if they will only believe. They preach that if you aren't healed, it's because of sin in your life or your lack of faith or both. Are they correct? Many of us want to believe that God still heals the sick. What does the Bible say about this teaching?

Why Is There Sickness?

The ninth chapter of John records Jesus' healing of a man born blind. Before Jesus gave sight to this poor soul, the disciples asked Him: ". . . Rabbi, who sinned, this man or his parents, that he should be born blind?" (John 9:2.) Their question reveals that they believed sickness to be a result of sin. It was the doctrine held among the rabbis of Israel, and it is an Eastern religious concept today: If you are sick, either you sinned, or it is a judgment upon your parents' sin. This attitude has infiltrated Christian thinking, although there is no biblical basis for the idea.[1]

The Scriptures devote an entire book of the Bible to refuting this notion. Job's friends all tried to convince poor Job that his afflictions could be removed, if he'd just repent! They were wrong. Jesus refuted this reasoning, ". . . It was neither that this man sinned, nor his parents . . ." (John 9:3). Where do so many modern faith healers get the idea that God wants all sickness healed?

The Healing Ministry of Jesus

Those who claim that God wants you well and all sickness can and should be healed like to point out that Jesus' healing ministry was all-inclusive. They refer to the Gospel records which repeatedly say: ". . . all who had any sick with various diseases brought them to Him; and laying His hands on *every one* of them, He was healing them" (Luke 4:40, *italics added*). ". . . and He healed *all* who were ill" (Matthew 8:16, *italics added*). ". . . and great multitudes were gathered to hear Him and to be healed of their sicknesses" (Luke 5:15). ". . . for power was coming from Him and healing them *all*" (Luke 6:19, *italics added*).

This last phrase, ". . . healing them all" is used to affirm that Jesus did not exclude any from His healing touch. Thus, all sickness should be healed today. If you are sick, you shouldn't be; God doesn't want you that way, or so the argument goes.

I often wish some of life's complicated issues could be dismissed so easily. However, sickness, health, and faith healing are a bit more complex than just "believe and be healed."

So in answer to the question, "Does God want to heal all sickness?" we first need to see what the Bible says about sickness. The Scriptures give us five basic reasons for sickness.

NATURAL AGING. In Hebrews 9:27, we read, "And inasmuch as it is appointed for men to die once, and after this comes judgment." We have an appointment to keep. All humanity must keep this appointment. We must die. This fact is the result of Adam's and Eve's sin in the beginning. We die because of the curse of death upon all nature. Sickness is often a natural symptom of the aging process. It is a part of the life process to bring us the next life. Science calls this process the Second Law of Thermodynamics. Everything is subject to bondage and decay (Romans 8:20–22). So, some sickness is a symptom of death, a direct result of Adam's fall in the Garden.

Slowing the process. A further word is needed here. It is true that indirectly all sickness and death are the result of sin—Adam's sin. Had our first parents never sinned, there would be no sickness or death. Because of Adam's sin, both Christians and unbelievers grow old and die. This is true no matter how much faith you have or whether or not you are healed of some sickness. We can slow the process, but we can't break our appointment; we all must die.

We can slow the process through proper diet and exercise, but we cannot escape the process. During the Exodus, God promised Israel that "none of these diseases" of the Egyptian world would come upon them if they would obey His teachings regarding diet. There is a well-documented book by a medical doctor who shows how the aging process and sickness can be deterred through obeying God's Word in our eating habits.[2]

SICKNESS AS A DIRECT RESULT OF SIN. In John 9, the man born blind had not committed a sin which caused his blindness, nor had his parents. However, some sickness and disease are the direct result of sin. Some children are born blind because of venereal disease in the mother. Her sin caused the blindness in the child.[3] The Bible makes it clear that not all sickness is the direct result of sin, but some is. In fact, in the Decalogue, where God gives His Law to Israel, Jehovah God warns that the sins of the parents are passed down to the third and fourth generation (Exodus 20:5). This can be further illustrated by a child who is born a heroin addict because his mother passed her addiction into the bloodstream of her child.

Unconfessed sin and sickness. Some sickness is caused by unconfessed sin in our lives. Unconfessed sin affects our physical health drastically. Much psychosomatic illness has a spiritual source. In the eleventh chapter of 1 Corinthians, Paul asserts that some Christians were sick as the result of abusing the ordinance of the Lord's Supper. Their sickness was a judgment of God upon them because of this unconfessed sin. He even says some had died! (1 Corinthians 11:30.)

Be anxious for nothing. Every doctor knows that inner anxiety can cause a multitude of physical ills. Inner peace produces freedom from those illnesses caused by guilt, fear, and other anxieties.[4]

James 5:14–16 links unconfessed sin with sickness. James tells the sick to confess all known sin before seeking healing from the hands of the elders. Indeed much sickness could be healed or prevented if we just stopped the sin that caused it. Drunkenness is a sin; it is also a sickness. It destroys the body. Stop the drinking, and you stop the sickness, if it has not done permanent damage. Many other illustrations could be given, but are not necessary. Some sickness is the direct result of sin.

DEMONIC ILLNESS. The Gospels record a number of experiences in the healing ministry of Christ in which He encountered sickness caused by demons. Whether or not you believe in demons is beside the point, Jesus did! He knew that some sickness is Satanic. Therefore, in order to heal the sick, He had to defeat the devil. Luke records such a healing in the thirteenth chapter of his Gospel. Jesus met a woman who, ". . . for eighteen years had had a sickness caused by a spirit; and she was bent double, and could not straighten up at all" (Luke 13:11). Curvature of the spine caused by a spirit. It's interesting to observe that when Jesus healed her, He laid hands on her and declared, ". . . Woman, you are freed from your sickness" (Luke 13:12). Notice, ". . . you are freed . . . ." Her sickness was a bondage caused by a demon.

Luke doesn't tell us how she got this demonic illness; he only reports that Satan caused it. Yes, she was instantly healed and straightened up. Why? Because the demon of sickness had fled.

Does it happen today? I am frequently asked if such demon-caused disease still occurs today. Yes, it does. I have seen such sickness and its deliverance; although it is more prevalent in pagan lands, where witchcraft and idolatry are common. Even the Apostle Paul felt that his physical affliction (he called it his "thorn in the flesh") was a messenger from Satan to torment him (*see* 2 Corinthians 12:7). Just what he meant by that is not clear, but it is clear that he felt Satan was responsible for his sickness.[5]

SICKNESS AS A SOURCE OF HOLINESS. Since we've mentioned Paul's thorn, a further study of this passage in 2 Corinthians 12 teaches us a fourth reason for sickness. Paul says he prayed three times for God to heal him. God's answer was *no*. God said to Paul, ". . . My grace is sufficient for you, for power is perfected in weakness . . ." (2 Corinthians 12:9). Here is a valuable lesson for us. God allowed Paul's sickness to continue to humble him, to keep him from exalting himself. Through his affliction, Paul learned to trust God. His illness was used by God to perfect his holiness. So it often is with us. Through trial and adversity, we learn things about God and His provision that we could not have learned any other way. ". . . He disciplines us for our good, that we may share His holiness" (Hebrews 12:10).

Are you one of those "proud spirits"? Paul was. He was prone to be self-sufficient and to exalt himself. Sometimes God allows disease, illness, and so on to come to us to humble our spirits until we cry out to Him and Him alone as our life source. The illness then becomes the tool to get our attention and thus makes us better Christians.

Also, sickness can be used to help others. As the one who is ill learns to trust God, he or she in turn can comfort others in their affliction (*see* 2 Corinthians 1:4). You have to walk a mile in another man's moccasins before you really understand his hurts. Here is a very clear teaching that rather than heal all illness, God chooses to use some illness to develop our spirits.

This is a good place to discuss a few other biblical instances when God could have healed sickness and did not. Paul left his friend Trophimus behind at Miletus, because he was too ill to travel. Why didn't Paul heal him? He could have. Wasn't Trophimus at least as good a Christian as some today who report instant healing? My reply is that both Paul and Trophimus discerned that healing was not the will of God at that time.

Paul told Timothy to drink a little wine for his ailing stomach (1 Timothy 5:23). This was a medicinal healing, revealing that Paul did not exclude medicine as a means of healing. Neither did our Lord Jesus. In healing the man born blind, Jesus made a mud pack for his eyes and put it on them. Why? Jesus could have spoken the word, and the man would have instantly received his sight. Why the mud packs? The only reason I can deduce is that it was an object lesson. There is healing in a mud pack. For centuries primitive men have known the value of mud put upon a wound. Was this our Lord's endorsement that medicine was God ordained to heal the sick? I believe it was. We must remember that all healing is of God. Healing is a temporary reversal of the aging process. It is a miracle, and all real miracles are of God.[6] God can heal through doctors or without them: That is His choice to make, not ours!

SOME SICKNESS IS TO BE HEALED THAT GOD MIGHT BE GLORIFIED. Here is the fifth biblical statement about sickness. The experience of healing in John 9 is a direct teaching that God allows some sickness for the very purpose that He might miraculously heal it. The blind man's blindness had nothing to do with anyone's sin, except Adam's. It was not a discipline or judgment. Listen to Jesus' statement as to why he was blind. ''It was neither that this man sinned, nor his parents, but it was in order that the works of God might be displayed in him, we must work the works of Him who sent me, as long as it is day; night is coming when no man can work.'' [7] Did you understand that? He was born blind that Jesus might heal him! Had he not been born blind we would not have the ninth chapter of John in our Scriptures. His healing becomes our blessing, centuries later.

God Is Sovereign

Don't ask me to explain the mind of God. Some of His thoughts are beyond us. You can count on this: God answers to no one. He is sovereign. He heals whom He wants to. When it fits into His divine purpose, He will heal. When sickness can be used to His glory, He chooses not to heal. This is why I feel we must reject the teaching of those who tell us God wants to heal *all* sickness. This simply is not biblical teaching. However, there are times when our Father chooses to heal—instantly, supernaturally, and gloriously. When that happens, He is glorified.

Beware of False Healing

A word of warning is in order! Not all healing is of God. There is such a thing as demonic healing. Satan can temporarily heal. All real healing is of God, but Satan can produce psychic healing. Some of what passes off as healing by faith healers is in this category. Have you noticed that the kind of healings that are claimed are in the marginal areas? You don't see many claims of healing for terminal cancer or other fatal diseases. Healings are mostly in the areas of emotional disorders or crippling diseases like arthritis. Not all those who claim healing are healed or stay healed.[8] The questions might be raised, "Why would Satan heal someone? If healing is a good thing, why would the devil do a good thing?" Again, all *real* healing is of God. Psychic or demonic healing only appears to be a healing. Often Satan will work his miracle through his servant in order to deceive the one being healed. He will heal the body in order to enslave the soul through false and cultic teaching. It has been observed that witch doctors in primitive religions can heal. They do so through demonic power. Remember, even Pharaoh's sorcerers could match Moses' miracles. Many a person has been led away from biblical Christianity by those who practiced healing from a nonscriptural basis.

Keep Your Hands Off Me
It is even possible to become demonized through the laying on of hands by those who practice demonic healing.[9] Not every healing is the touch of Jesus, even though it is done in His name. I suggest you be very careful whom you let lay hands on you for healing. We are often impressed and emotionally carried away by the apparent results of those who practice mass-healing meetings. Some of these may be of God; some may not. How can you tell the true from the false? A few questions might help.

- Are his teachings scriptural regarding healing? If he claims that God wants everyone well and free of sickness, watch out.
- Are his methods of healing scriptural? James 5:14–16 is a New Testament pattern for healing. Healing is a church ministry. It is a part of the Body Life and gifts of the gathered church. I question whether the methods used by some preachers fit these biblical guidelines.
- Does the healer practice "slaying in the spirit"? No doubt you have seen this done. The healer touches the person needing healing, and the person faints or collapses or both! This is called slaying in the spirit. Now the question is: Which spirit did the slaying? I have searched the Scriptures over and over, and I find absolutely no basis for this practice. Admittedly it is sensational, but is it scriptural? I

fear not. I personally would fear for my own soul's security if such a thing happened to me. This type of method is common practice among witch doctors and primitive religions of the world. According to Kurt Koch, the world-reknowned authority on witchcraft, such practices constitute magic and have no place in a New Testament church.[10] I have no desire to be negative or to put down anyone's ministry. The Bible does teach us to pray for the sick, that they may be healed. However, we must also be wise and discerning, lest we be misled. Even as I write this, the world has been shocked by the reports of nearly one thousand people who committed religious mass suicide in Guyana, South America, under the leadership of Reverend Jim Jones. In the name of Christianity, this demonic, terrible deed was done.

The Real and the False
How can we discern real healing from demonic, psychic, or otherwise fraudulent healing? Two criteria have been suggested:

- Is the motive for healing the glory of God? (John 9:3.)
- The end result will be the lordship of Christ in the healed person's life (John 9:38).

The incidents of miracles and healing in the ministry of Jesus were all signs of His deity. They were road signs that declared His messiahship. He healed the body to save the soul. This is still His fundamental purpose in healing.

A Church Ministry
Because God does desire to heal the sick in special instances, the New Testament church should be involved in this ministry. In fact, the church is the *only* one who should be in this ministry. It is a church ministry, not some self-proclaimed healer's ministry. Healing is a gift given to the Body of Christ (1 Corinthians 12:9) and is to be exercised by the elders of the church. James 5:14–16 is to be our pattern for this healing ministry. It is my personal opinion that if more congregations and denominations were open to this pattern of

healing ministry, then fewer people would, in desperation, go running to other sources for help. Our failure to be open to the supernatural has robbed thousands of this vital touch from Jesus.

How to Pray for Healing

A practical word would be helpful here. Suppose you or someone you love is sick. How can you find the mind of God on this sickness? Let me suggest some steps of action:

1. *Search your heart for sin or unbelief.* Could the sickness be the result of unconfessed or unyielded sin? Could it be a judgment of God upon you to bring you to repentance? Search your heart; seek His face; turn from any and all sin He shows you. "[If] . . . My people who are called by My name . . . turn from their wicked ways, then I will hear from heaven . . . and will heal their land" (2 Chronicles 7:14).

2. *Ask God what He's trying to teach you.* After repentance, when you are sure that all is right before God, ask Him what you can learn through this. At first, don't ask for healing; ask for wisdom! Better to meet God in sickness than to miss Him in health! After you have a peace in your heart that you have trusted your need to Him, regardless of your state of being, you might seek healing.

3. *Call for the elders to pray for healing.* According to James 5, seek those who have a walk with God to pray for God's will and way in this illness. Now, how should the elders pray?

- *Pray until healing comes.* "Ask and keep on asking, seek and keep on seeking, knock and keep on knocking" (*see* Luke 11:9).
- *Pray until you get the assurance healing will come.* Sometimes, before healing actually comes, God tells our spirits He is going to heal. At this point our prayer becomes, "Thank You, Jesus, for what You are going to do."

- *Pray until God says, "No."* When God tells you it is not His will to heal, then your prayer must become, "Father, Thy will be done."
- *Seek His grace.* When God doesn't heal, He gives something every bit as wonderful: His sustaining grace! His presence is all-sufficient. James 4:6 says, "[He] . . . gives grace to the humble."

Faith Is the Key

One last word here. Often the key that unlocks the door to heaven's blessings is our faith. Every problem in our Christian life ultimately is a faith problem. We must believe God. As it is according to our faith, so is it. Once we know the mind of God regarding sickness and healing, our position is to be that of trusting reliance upon Him. Faith in God and His Word is the key to all God has for us.

Source Notes

1. Watchman Nee, in his three-volume work *The Spiritual Man,* holds to the idea that sickness is the direct result of sin. Watchman Nee, *The Spiritual Man,* Vol. 3 (New York: Christian Fellowship Publishers, 1968).
2. S. I. McMillin, *None of These Diseases* (Old Tappan, NJ: Fleming H. Revell, 1963).
3. Not all those afflicted with venereal disease are to be classified as sinners, because not all venereal disease is spread sexually.
4. See Dr. McMillin's rather extensive discussion on the effects of anxiety on health in *None of These Diseases.*
5. Some persons have taught that Paul was demonized with a demon of sickness. This argument is based on the word *angel.* Since a demon is a fallen angel, the reasoning is that Paul's messenger was a fallen angel: a demon. This is fanciful interpretation, since Paul's thorn was in his flesh, not his spirit. Demons are never called angels in the apostles' writings.
6. This statement could be challenged. Satan can and does work miracles. The Antichrist will work wonders and signs (2 Thessalonians 2:8).

7. G. Campbell Morgan, in his commentary on this passage, translates the verse in this fashion. In the original language, there is no punctuation. It has to be supplied by the translators. Morgan felt that the period after *parents* gave it the best meaning. This would imply that the work that Jesus and the disciples would do would bring about the working of the will of God. Morgan did not accept the idea that the man had been born blind in order to show what Jesus could do with him. G. Campbell Morgan, *The Gospel According to John* (Old Tappan, NJ: Fleming H. Revell), pp. 162–170.

8. William A. Nolen, *Healing: A Doctor in Search of a Miracle* (NY: Random House, 1974).

9. Merrill F. Unger, *Demons in the World Today* (Wheaton, IL: Tyndale House, 1971). See chapter seven, "Demons and Healing," pp. 125 ff.

10. Kurt Koch, *The Devil's Alphabet* (Grand Rapids, MI: Kregel Pubns., 1969). See chapter twenty-five, "Magical Healing Methods," pp. 75 ff.

Additional Reading

Kelsey, Morton. *Healing and Christianity: In Ancient Thought and Modern Times*. NY: Harper & Row, 1976. This is the newest and most complete book on the subject.

Koch, Kurt E. *Between Christ and Satan*. (Grand Rapids, MI: Kregel Pubns., 1962). See chapter five, "Miracles of Healing Today," pp. 142–152.

8 *How Can I Learn to Pray?*

Praying is the most important thing we do in our Christian life. Because prayer opens the door to heaven's blessings, Satan continually seeks to defeat our prayer fellowship with the Father. It would be interesting to ask 100 Christians, at random, how they rate the effectiveness of their praying. I suspect that the majority of those questioned would feel very ineffective in prayer. Believers today cry out like the disciples of old, "Lord, teach us to pray . . ." (Luke 11:1).

Why Should I Learn to Pray?

New Christians often don't know where to begin in learning how to pray. Oftentimes we fail to understand the importance of prayer. Someone once said that the most important thing one Christian can do for another Christian is to teach him how to pray. Prayer is vital to fellowship with God, and fellowship with God is the most vital thing in life. Let me begin with some basic reasons why we should learn to pray. First, praying is talking to God. It is communication with our Father. Prayer needs no special religious or holy language. Prayer is simply talking to your Father in heaven. It is the talking part of your relationship with God. You can speak to God, your Father, as you would talk to your earthly father. You are His son or daughter, and you speak to Him out of that relationship (Romans 8:15).

Second, there should be a strong motivation to pray. When a person tells me that he has no basic desire to communicate with his heavenly Father, then that tells me some very definite things about that person. It seems to me that every true believer, by his very nature, will desire to pray. This is true because everywhere there is life there is evidence of life. When life exists there are such evidences as hunger, thirst, activity, and desire. A true believer has God's life within him. The indwelling Holy Spirit creates an inner compulsion to pray. ". . . for we do not know how to pray as we should, but the Spirit Himself intercedes for us with groanings too deep for words" (Romans 8:26).

We should learn to pray because we desire to fellowship with God, since we are truly His children.

We should pray because our Saviour commanded us to pray. He said we, ". . . ought to pray and not to lose heart" (Luke 18:1). At all times we are to pray ". . . without ceasing" (1 Thessalonians 5:17). We must keep in constant touch with Jesus in order to be what He wants us to be.

We should pray because praying is a characteristic of a normal, healthy Christian experience. Jesus tells us, "If you abide in Me, and My words abide in you, ask whatever you wish, and it shall be done for you" (John 15:7). A disciple is one who abides, brings forth fruit, and gets his prayers answered!

There is another reason why we must learn to pray. This reason is fundamental to pleasing Jesus with our daily living. In John 14:12 are recorded these words of Christ to us, "Truly, truly, I say to you, he who believes in Me, the works that I do shall he do also; and greater works than these shall he do; because I go to the Father." What a remarkable statement! Jesus says every believer is to do two miraculous things:

- *Equal* His works: ". . . the works that I do shall he do also . . . ."
- *Exceed* His works: ". . . and greater works than these shall he do . . . ."

Remarkably, Jesus expects us to live supernaturally, doing greater miracles than He did. Wow! Now, how in the world can that be? All right, listen! He tells us how to live miraculously in the following verses of this exciting passage. Verses thirteen and fourteen continue, "And whatever you ask in My name, that will I do, that the Father may be glorified in the Son. If you ask Me anything in My name, I will do it." Jesus tells us the key to miraculous living is through the power of prayer in His name. This is a very good reason for learning how to pray.[1] Did you notice that our prayers put Jesus to work? He said, "You ask, and I will do." Isn't that fantastic? My prayers put Jesus to work on my behalf. How exciting! Lord, teach us to pray!

Real Praying

Learning to pray is not difficult, if you understand the role the Holy Spirit plays in prayer. Four times, in Scripture, the Holy Spirit is mentioned in connection with mighty praying.

- The Holy Spirit is called, ". . . the Spirit of grace and supplication . . ." (Zechariah 12:10).
- In Jude 20 we are told to pray in the Holy Spirit.
- Paul encourages us to ". . . pray at all times in the Spirit . . ." (Ephesians 6:18).
- And finally, we are told how the Holy Spirit can help us learn to pray: "And in the the same way the Spirit also helps our weakness; for we do not know how to pray as we should, but the Spirit Himself intercedes for us with groanings too deep for words; and He who searches the hearts knows what the mind of the Spirit is, because He intercedes for the saints according to the will of God" (Romans 8:26, 27).

These four passages urge us to pray in the Holy Spirit. What is real prayer? Genuine communication with God is praying in the Holy Spirit. A prayer that is motivated by, energized, sustained, and empowered by the Holy Spirit will get through to God and bless your life and the lives of others.

As a believer, it is more important to learn to pray in the Spirit than it is to learn to preach in the Spirit. Spirit-led praying is more needful than Spirit-led teaching, witnessing, or evangelism. Learning to pray in the power of God's Spirit is the test of your growth in godliness.

With or *In* the Spirit

As we learn to pray, it should be observed that praying *in* the Spirit is not the same as praying *with* the Spirit. Paul, in 1 Corinthians 14:15, mentions his own praying with the spirit. A careful reading of these verses reveals that Paul was referring, not to the Holy Spirit, but rather with his own human spirit. Praying with the spirit seems to be a reference to praying in a tongue. Praying in the Spirit has to do with Holy Spirit-empowered praying.

Our Helplessness

In Romans 8:26 the apostle says most of us don't know how to pray as we should. Therefore, God's Holy Spirit who indwells us, wants to help our weakness in prayer. The word translated *weakness* in the New American Standard Version is translated *infirmities* in the King James Version. This is incorrect. The word should be singular and not plural. The New American Standard Version translates it correctly, *weakness*. What is our one great weakness that the Holy Spirit must help us with? Romans 8:8 tells us, ". . . those who are in the flesh cannot please God." What that means is that you and I, in our own strength, can never live the Christian life. Our *flesh* (the self life) can never please God. We need the Holy Spirit's power in us. A friend of mine has an axiom of the Christian life that he says every Christian should live by. His axiom of life is: I am totally unable to do anything in and of myself in the spiritual realm. That is the weakness Paul was affirming. Now, apply that axiom to prayer. Are you aware of your total inability to pray in your own strength? Well, learn it. The first step in learning to pray is learning you can't pray without God's Spirit to help you. When you have learned this truth, God has you right where He wants you. As long as you and I think we can pray, preach, teach, witness, and live in our own strength, then the Holy Spirit cannot manifest His power.

The Helper in Our Praying

In what way can the Holy Spirit help us pray? First of all, He prompts us and puts the desire in us to pray. Remember, Zechariah calls the Spirit of God the Spirit of supplication. It is the very nature of the Spirit to pray. No wonder He can help us desire to pray. If you lack the desire to pray, just get yourself rightly related to the Holy Spirit. When the Holy Spirit is in control of your life, you'll want to pray often. It is worthy of note that praying isn't always a talking communication. Sometimes the Spirit in us will prompt us to seek fellowship with God the Father, just because the Father wants to be with us. Fellowship isn't always speaking; sometimes it's just being together.

What to Say

New believers and others who are learning to pray frequently remark that it is difficult to know what to say to God in prayer. "I just can't think of what to say," I've heard people say. Romans 8:26 tells us that the Holy Spirit gives us the content of our prayer, because when we pray in the Spirit, the Holy Spirit Himself actually does the praying and makes intercession. Therefore, when we are filled with the Spirit, our prayers actually become the Holy Spirit praying through us. He makes utterances for us (*see* Romans 8:26).

If this sounds strange to you, let me remind you that we believe this about other spiritual pursuits. We speak of a man preaching in the Spirit, and we say God is speaking through him. We speak of Spirit-led witnessing, teaching, and so forth. Then we should learn to pray in the Spirit! He'll give us God's words, God's feelings, God's emotions. He'll pray through us with groanings too deep for words. Also, He'll always pray according to the will of God, which guarantees your prayer will be answered (1 John 5:14).

Suppose someone asks you to pray for something, and you're not sure it's God's will. I've heard folks handle this by praying, "God, if it's Your will . . . ." I've always felt that was an escape clause, in case the prayer wasn't answered. Granted, there are times when we must simply pray, "Thy will be done," as Jesus did in His hour of agony. Yet, at times of not knowing God's will, the Holy Spirit can help us.

How to Pray in the Spirit

In conclusion, here are some practical aids to praying. In order to allow the Holy Spirit to control your praying, I suggest you:

- Begin by confessing your sins up-to-date.
- Then choose against self and submit to God's will. James 4:7 says, "Submit therefore to God . . . ."
- Ask God to forbid Satan to interfere in your prayer time. Take authority over the enemy in Jesus' name.
- Willingly ask the Holy Spirit to take control of your spirit, mind,

and will. Tell the Spirit you want Him to pray through you.
• Then wait on the Lord for an impression. Begin by just praising God; perhaps reading a praise psalm back to the Father from His Word. Then, as the Holy Spirit gives you words and thoughts, pray them to the throne of grace. "Delight yourself in the Lord; And He will give you the desires of your heart" (Psalms 37:4).

Claiming a Promise

When you are praying for something that God has clearly promised in His Word, it is not necessary to beg and plead with Him to keep His word. I suggest you pray in this fashion:

• Remind God of His promise. Quote His Word to Him. Let Him know you believe His Word.
• Bring your need before Him.
• Claim it by faith. "Father, I believe Your promise. I claim it as my own as Your child." Mark 11:24 reads, ". . . all things for which you pray and ask, believe that you have received them, and they shall be granted you."
• Then praise Him and continue thanking Him for the answer; it's on the way. Leave the how, the when, and the where of the answer up to God.

Thou are coming to a King
Large petitions with thee bring
For His grace and power are such
None can ever ask too much.

JOHN NEWTON

Source Notes
1. There are really two keys to miraculous living. In the following verses, Jesus gives detailed teaching about the coming of the Holy Spirit to indwell the believer. Thus, through prayer and the Holy Spirit's power in us, we can equal and exceed the ministry of Jesus Himself.

Additional Reading
Gordon, S. D. *Quiet Talks on Prayer.* NY: Grosset & Dunlap, 1960.
The Kneeling Christian. Grand Rapids, MI: Zondervan, 1971, chapters 5, 6.

9 Why Doesn't God Answer My Prayers?

Every Christian needs to know more about the miracle and mystery of prayer. This is one area of Christian life in which we never have all the answers. Prayer is a person-to-God encounter and therefore is a profound experience. Prayer, real prayer, is where heaven and earth meet. It is a burning bush: Take off your shoes, you are on holy ground! Because praying is a divine encounter, its mysteries are measureless. God's Word gives us teaching and illustration regarding prayer, but real understanding only comes with experience.

Some of us have had only bad experiences with prayer. In fact, as I write this chapter, it was only last night that I talked to a young adult who said, "I prayed, but it went no higher than the ceiling." We've all felt that emotion! Prayer sometimes is like dialing a phone and getting a busy signal or being put on hold! That's frustrating, to say the least. The young adult I mentioned just had no confidence that God hears and answers prayer. He simply did not know how to "get through" to God.

Why No Answer?

Let me try to give some insight into this crucial need. Everyone needs to talk to our heavenly Father and needs to know He can and does answer our prayers. So, whenever a believer talks to God and seems to get no answer, why? Why is it that God doesn't always answer our prayers? This is a very real problem, and we need some light from the Scriptures on this matter of unanswered prayer, because he who keeps praying and getting no answer soon quits praying. And he who quits praying loses touch with God and misses life's source of power and blessing.[1]

Unanswered or Unoffered?

James 4:1–4 addresses itself to this problem of unanswered prayer:

> What is the source of quarrels and conflicts among you? Is not the source your pleasures that wage war in your members? You lust and do not have; so you commit murder. And you are envious and cannot obtain; so you fight and quarrel. You do not have because you do not ask. You ask and do not receive, because you ask with wrong motives, so that you may spend it on your pleasures. You adulteresses, do you not know that friendship with the world is hostility toward God? Therefore whoever wishes to be a friend of the world makes himself an enemy of God.

Did you notice that these verses mention several problems affecting our prayer life? Even though unanswered prayer is a problem, there is a greater problem. James says in verse two, ". . . You do not have because you do not ask." Unoffered prayer is our greatest prayer problem. You may wonder why God doesn't respond to you; but, believe me, God wonders why you don't talk to Him more often than you do! You can believe this: God, our Father, wants to answer more requests than we're willing to ask of Him. Jesus said regarding prayer, "Ask and it shall be given to you; seek, and you shall find; knock, and it shall be opened to you. For every one who asks receives . . ." (Matthew 7:7). God wants to answer our prayers. He desires for us to pray. We have not because we ask not.

When Prayer Doesn't Work

Yet, there are times when you do ask, and it may seem, at the time, that prayer doesn't work. When that happens, James, the brother of our Lord offers us some suggestions why. Whenever our prayers seem not to get through, we need to find what hinders the answers. James suggests we look in three directions.

LOOK AT YOURSELF. Our prayers are like a missile that is launched into the heavens. A missile is no more successful than the platform from which it is launched. Our lives are the platforms from which prayer is lifted up to the Father. When we pray, God first looks at the "pray-er," before He listens to the prayer itself. It's the life that prays. Therefore the failure of our prayer to get through may be due to the manner of life we are living. James 4:1–4 describes a life of worldliness. In verse 4, James says, "You adulteresses, do you not know that friendship with the world is hostility toward God? . . ." Our sin can hinder answered prayer. "But your iniquities have made a separation between you and your God, And your sins have hid His face from you, so that He does not hear" (Isaiah 59:2). The Psalmist declared, "If I regard wickedness in my heart, the Lord will not hear" (Psalms 66:18). Notice the phrase "The Lord will not hear." The Psalmist equated refusal to hear with refusal to answer. God hears all our prayers. Sometimes He just refuses to answer. At other times He just says, "No," and that is His answer.

Therefore, if prayer seems not to work, first examine your heart before God. A pure heart opens the door to God's blessings. First John 3:21, 22 says: "Beloved, if our heart does not condemn us, we have confidence before God; and whatever we ask we receive from Him, because we keep His commandments and do the things that are pleasing in His sight." These verses tell us to obey, and our prayers will be answered. God looks at an obedient life before He listens to the prayer. The verb *keep* is in the Greek present tense which indicates a continual habit of life. Thus the Christian who continually lives in obedience can ask whatever he will, and he shall receive, but the believer who only occasionally obeys does not have such a guarantee of answered prayer . . . .

James 5:16 tells us: ". . . The effective prayer of a *righteous* man can accomplish much" (*italics added*).

As God looks at our lives, He examines our unforgiving spirits. Jesus taught much about prayer and forgiveness. Continually Jesus links the two together. In the Sermon on the Mount He tells us, "If therefore you are presenting your offering at the altar, and there remember that your brother has something against you, leave your offering there before the altar, and go your way; first be reconciled to your brother, and then come and present your offering'' (Matthew 5:23, 24). He reaffirms this in what we call the Lord's Prayer. "Forgive us our trespasses as we forgive those who trespass against us." Here then is a great principle: You must forgive in order to be forgiven. Bitterness in your heart hinders God from answering prayer.

Sometimes God looks at our motive in prayer. "You ask and do not receive, because you ask with wrong motives . . ." says James 4:3. Have you ever prayed for something out of a selfish motive? Sure you have. Who hasn't? James says God is not going to answer that kind of praying, so we can go spend it on our pleasures.

I once had a woman ask me to pray for her husband to be saved; then, before I could say I would, she continued, "I've been praying for my husband to be saved, because I can't drive, and every Sunday I have to ride to church with friends and then sit in a couples' Sunday-school class. And I'm the only one there without a husband. It's very embarrassing." It doesn't take a wise man to see that her motives weren't too noble!

Wrong motives hinder God's response. Suppose you are praying for a raise in pay, but you are not honoring God now with the money you have. Why should God give you a raise? To do so would only promote your stealing more money from Him! God does look at the manner of our living and the motive of our praying. The only prayer Jesus didn't answer was that of the impenitent thief on the cross. "If You are the Son of God, save Yourself and us," he cried. His motives were impure, and Jesus ignored him. There is a motive that honors God and pleases Him. Jesus said, "And whatever you ask in My name, that will I do, *that the Father may be glorified in the Son*" (John 14:13, *italics added*).

LOOK AT YOUR PRAYER. If your life and motives are right, what about your prayer? Is it right? Is your prayer in line with God's will? Every prayer prayed according to the will of God gets God's immediate attention.

First John 5:14, 15 tells us: "And this is the confidence which we have before Him, that, if we ask anything according to His will, He hears us. And if we know that He hears us in whatever we ask, we

know that we have the requests which we have asked from Him."
What a glorious truth for those who have lost confidence in prayer!
If only we could pray according to God's will, then we could know
the answer is on the way. We *have* (present tense) the requests we
desired of Him.

Some have observed that faith is what really makes prayer work.
They quote Jesus' words, ". . . all things for which you pray and
ask, *believe* that you have received them, and they shall be granted
you" (Mark 11:24, *italics added*). Faith is important to experiencing
power in prayer, but all the faith in the world will not get an answer
to a prayer that is outside the will of God. This is true in regard to
miraculous healing. I've seen folks continually believe that God
would heal their loved one, then they've watched that precious life
die! [2] You see, faith must be founded upon the facts of the Word of
God. It is not a fact that God's Word teaches that He wants to heal
all sickness. Sometimes what we call faith is nothing more than the
power of positive thinking. Faith is more than just believing in our
believing. The great issue is not faith, but the sovereign will of God.
When my prayer falls in line with God's eternal purposes, then, and
only then, can I have boldness before the throne of grace (Hebrews
4:16).

My will or His: That's the question. How can we be sure? No
Spirit-filled Christian would deliberately ask for something he knew
was not God's will. Yet we often do pray from wrong motives and
selfish desires. How can this be corrected? I am convinced there are
no foolproof guarantees. Even Paul prayed three times for his thorn
in the flesh to be removed, not knowing this wasn't God's will [3] (2
Corinthians 12:7). However, there are some guidelines I've found
helpful. First, I must have a yielded life before God—sins confessed
up-to-date. Second, I request the Holy Spirit to have full control of
thought and deed. Third, I must search the Scriptures for light on the
request, to see if it's contrary to biblical truth. Fourth, I pray until
He answers or until I get the assurance He's going to answer. Finally
He may say, "No." Then all I can pray is, "Thy will be done."

LOOK TO GOD. Wait a minute; don't give up yet! There is more here
than we've discussed. Who can know the mind of our great God?

His thoughts are not ours. In years of learning what prayer is and how to pray effectively, I've learned yet another aspect of prayer not being answered. Often the delay is not due to sin, selfishness, an unforgiving spirit, or the will of God. Sometimes the problem is not with us or our prayer, but rather with God Himself. Look at yourself, look at your prayer, then look to God.

A different answer. Sometimes God *is* answering your prayer, but He is answering it differently from the way you desired. This was true of Paul's prayer for God to remove his thorn, as I mentioned. Paul wanted it healed; God wanted to use it to teach Paul valuable lessons of dependence upon His grace. When God answers your requests differently, you just have to trust Him. You know: Father knows best. You may have wanted a *yes* reply and got a *no*. Well, no *is* an answer; isn't it?

A delayed answer. Sometimes God delays the answer, and we mistake the delay for a *no* answer. Our schedule of reply doesn't always match His. You prayed a prayer months ago, and because the answer didn't come when you wanted it to, you thought your heavenly Father didn't care about you and your needs. He may have been at work all the time! Even while you slept, He was working in answer to your prayer. Even when you had forgotten what you prayed, He was answering.

Do you recall who Zacharias was? He was the father of John the Baptist. Now that's his claim to fame. It took a miraculous answer to prayer to bring that to pass. Zacharias, a priest in the temple at Jerusalem, had no children. His wife, Elizabeth, was barren. Luke records it in his Gospel. ''And they had no child, because Elizabeth was barren, and they were both advanced in years'' (Luke 1:7). In his old age, as he was going about his temple duties one day, God sent an angel to him with a message. The message was a strange one. It had to do with a delayed answer to prayer. The angel said, ''Do not be afraid, Zacharias, [the angel had a sense of humor because the previous verse describes the terror that came over the old priest at seeing an angel in the temple!] for your petition has been heard, and your wife Elizabeth will bear you a son, and you will give him the name John'' (Luke 1:13).

Old Zacharias was shocked at the message. Why? Because the angel said he had come in response to his prayer. What prayer? Zacharias had not prayed for a son in years. He had given up on that petition many hugs and kisses ago! He and Elizabeth figured God had said *no* to their youthful prayer. Here is a great principle for us to learn about prayers. God may delay the answer in order to answer it with something better than what we prayed for. Zacharias and his wife requested a son and got a prophet! And what a prophet he was: John the Baptist! You see, often God has more in store for us than we have for ourselves!

Angels and our prayers. There is another reason some answers are delayed. God may have answered your prayer immediately, only to have the answer delayed in transmission. In the previously cited illustration of Zacharias, the priest in the temple, God sent the mighty angel Gabriel as a messenger to relay His answer to Zacharias. There is another biblical passage which refers to an angel coming in direct answer to prayer. In Daniel 10 we are told that Daniel had been in prayer and fasting for three weeks. At the end of that period, Daniel saw a man in a vision (in reality it was an angel) who had been sent by God in answer to Daniel's prayer.[3] The angel touched Daniel and gave him this strange message: ". . . O Daniel, man of high esteem, understand the words that I am about to tell you and stand upright, for I have now been sent to you . . . . Do not be afraid, Daniel, for from the first day that you set your heart on understanding this and humbling yourself before your God, your words were heard, and I have come in response to your words" (Daniel 10:11, 12). Before we continue to quote this angel, I want you to note again his words, "from the first day." Daniel had been praying for twenty-one days, and the angel had been traveling twenty-one days! Now, either heaven is a long way off, or that was some *slow* angel! Not really! There is a third explanation for the delay. Let's read on. "But the prince of the kingdom of Persia was withstanding me for twenty-one days; then behold, Michael, one of the chief princes, came to help me, for I had been left there with the kings of Persia" (Daniel 10:13).

What are we to make of this statement? The references to princes in verse thirteen are references to angels and Satan. The prince of Persia is an allusion to Satan.[4] Michael, the archangel, is a prince of God. Here then, is a startling conclusion. Daniel prayed a prayer. Twenty-one days passed before an answer came. An angel appeared and told Daniel he had been delayed because Satan hindered him. It took the intervention of a mightier angel, Michael himself, to win the battle. It's as though this angel had been kidnapped, detoured, and defeated, until Michael came to the rescue. All this was going on in the heavenlies while Daniel was praying! If we only knew what spiritual warfares are going on while we pray! So here is another reason some answers are delayed. Satan can hinder and delay the answer.

The Blessing of Unanswered Prayer

Have you ever asked God for something and later been thankful that He didn't answer your prayer? I don't know about you, but I've asked the Father for some rather stupid things that, at the time, I thought were good for me; and it turned out later I was wrong. Praise God for unanswered prayer! We need to believe that our heavenly Father only wants the best for us; therefore, if an answer is delayed, you can rely upon the fact that He will answer it in a better way. Paul said it well, "What then shall we say to these things? If God is for us, who is against us? He who did not spare His own Son, but delivered Him up for us all, how will He not also with Him freely give us all things?" (Romans 8:31, 32.)

God does answer prayer. Therefore, when you pray, believe an answer is on the way. It may be *yes;* it may be *no;* or it may be *wait;* but whatever the answer, it will be in your best interest. If it seems God is not listening, look at your life: Is it free from known sin? Look at your motive: Is it selfish? Look at your prayer: Is it according to God's will? Look to God: Is He delaying the answer or answering it differently?

Then keep praying. "Since then we have a great high priest who has passed through the heavens, Jesus the Son of God, let us hold fast our confession. For we do not have a high priest who cannot sympathize with our weaknesses, but one who has been tempted in all things as we are, yet without sin" (Hebrews 4:14, 15).

Unanswered yet? the prayer your lips have pleaded
  In agony of heart these many years?
Does faith begin to fail, is hope declining,
  And think you all in vain those falling tears?
Say not, the Father hath not heard your prayer,
  You shall have your desire sometime, somewhere.

Unanswered yet! Though when you first presented
  This one petition at the Father's Throne
It seemed you could not wait the time of asking,
  So urgent was the heart to make it known;
Though years have passed since then, do not despair,
  The Lord will answer you sometime, somewhere.

Unanswered yet! Nay, do not say ungranted,
  Perhaps your work is not wholly done.
The work began when first your prayer was uttered,
  And God will finish what He has begun.
If you will keep the incense burning there,
  His glory you shall see sometime, somewhere.

Unanswered yet? Faith cannot be unanswered,
  Her feet are firmly planted on the Rock;
Amid the wildest storms she stands undaunted,
  Nor quails before the loudest thunder shock,
She knows Omnipotence has heard her prayer,
  And cries, "It shall be done, sometime, somewhere."

MRS. OPHELIA G. BROWNING

Source Notes

1. S. D. Gordon, *Quiet Talks on Prayer* (New York: Grosset & Dunlap, 1960). See "Hindrances on Prayer," pp. 71–114.
2. See chapter seven, "Does God Want to Heal All Sickness?" for a full discussion of this subject.
3. The word *angel* literally means "messenger." One of the main purposes of angelic beings is to serve as the Father's messengers.
4. Biblical scholars differ on this point. The prince of Persia may be

an allusion to one of Satan's archdemons, rather than Satan himself. At any rate, the result is the same.

Additional Reading

Bounds, E. M. *Power Through Prayer*. Grand Rapids, MI: Baker Book House, 1962.

Chadwick, Samuel. *The Path of Prayer*. Fort Washington, PA: Christian Literature Crusade, 1951. See "The Problem of Unanswered Prayer," p. 89.

Goforth, Rosalind. *How I Know God Answers Prayer*. Chicago: Moody Press, 1800.

Gordon, S. D. *Quiet Talks on Prayer*. NY: Grosset & Dunlap, 1960.

Harrah, Allegra. *Prayer Weapons*. Old Tappan, NJ: Fleming H. Revell, 1976.

Prince, Derek. *Shaping History Through Prayer and Fasting*. Old Tappan, NJ: Fleming H. Revell, 1973.

Rinker, Rosalind. *Prayer: Conversing With God*. Grand Rapids, MI: Zondervan, 1974.

Torrey, R. A. *How to Pray*. Old Tappan, NJ: Fleming H. Revell, 1970.

Wallis, Arthur. *Pray in the Spirit*. Fort Washington, PA: Christian Literature Crusade, 1970.

10 Is Premarital Sex Always Wrong?

Being a Christian does not guarantee control over one's sexual appetites. The Christian couple in love faces the same temptations as an unbelieving couple. A very real question has to do with sex between single people. The statement one often hears is, "If we love each other and plan to be married soon, what can be wrong with sex before marriage?" Is premarital sex always wrong?

Rules and Principles

The Bible speaks directly about sexual immorality. The Apostle Paul, on a number of occasions, uses the expression, "flee fornication." [1] This word is the most common biblical word used to describe sexual intercourse between anyone outside of marriage. It describes any sexual immorality, but primarily the sex act itself among singles. The *Zondervan Topical Bible* defines *fornication* as "The unlawful sexual intercourse of an unwed person." Fornication is the biblical word used to describe what our society calls premarital sex. Jesus, Paul, and other New Testament writers say, "Flee from it." The problem comes when we find our feelings do not agree with God's commands. There is a phrase in Debby Boone's hit song, "You Light Up My Life," which says, "How can love be wrong when it feels so right?" Those words describe the feelings of thousands of young people today—even Christian couples who are involved in what God calls fornication: premarital sex. Yet many will tell you it's not wrong, at least not for them, because they are in love! According to the thinking of many couples, love justifies sexual oneness without marriage, because it is the natural expression of their affection.

Why Does God Say *Wait*?

Okay, is premarital sex really wrong even when it doesn't *feel* wrong? That's a fair question. Besides, why does God tell us to wait anyway? Some answers are needed. To begin with, every child of God needs to learn that behind each of God's laws, there is a moral principle. This moral principle is God's reason for giving the law. Our Father always has a reason or principle behind each of His laws. When God says "Thou shalt not . . ." He does so for at least two reasons. The first reason is to protect us and guide us. He desires to protect us from being hurt. He knows we don't break His laws so much as they break us! Second, He desires to guide us into a better relationship or experience. So, as we discuss "why wait till marriage?" let's consider several good principles, or reasons, for waiting until marriage to satisfy one's sexual desires.

A very obvious reason for waiting is simply because God says you should. An obedient Christian doesn't have to question God's motives for His prohibitions. Out of love and trust for our heavenly Father, we should just obey because we feel that Father knows best. He loves us and wants to protect and guide us.

Without a doubt, there are some happily married couples who had sexual intercourse before marriage. They might even testify that sex was a genuine expression of love and that they felt no guilt regarding their premarital sex life. Some would even declare that it relieved sexual tension during a long engagement and proved their sexual compatibility. However, the odds are against such a successful experience. Often premarital sex brings with it many negative results. Besides, God says it's sin, and sin is always less than God's best.

A major survey was taken to explore the idea that premarital sex improved a couple's sex life during marriage. The results were negative. Those who were virgins on their wedding night developed a sex life as good or better than those who were not. The survey revealed that some couples who had waited till marriage actually had a more meaningful sex life than those who did not. Therefore it is not true that couples need to try it out to see if they're compatible.[2]

Presuming Upon the Future

For every couple that has no adverse reactions to their fornication, there are many more who, in retrospect, wish they had waited. One reason God says ". . . abstain from fornication" (1 Thessalonians 4:3 KJV) is because it presumes upon the future. The Bible warns us, "Do not boast about tomorrow, For you do not know what a day may bring forth" (Proverbs 27:1). Jesus tells us not to be anxious about tomorrow, because today has enough troubles of its own (Matthew 6:34). The point is: God wants us to live one day at a time. The couple who decides to have sexual intercourse, with the idea that it is not wrong because they intend to marry, is presuming upon the future. Only God controls tomorrow. I know of two couples who planned to marry, had sex, only to have accidents claim the lives of the young men. Both young women expressed regrets that they were no longer virgins. They wished they had not assumed marriage would happen.

The Purpose of Dating

Another principle to consider is that sex between singles is a reversal of God's purpose for marriage and dating. I am often asked, "What constitutes marriage?" Does a piece of paper called a marriage license make a marriage in God's sight? This is an important question. Jesus said, ". . . For this cause a man shall leave his father and mother, and shall cleave to his wife; and the two shall because our flesh . . ." (Matthew 19:5). Notice what Christ declared as constituting a marriage union: "one flesh." Sexual intercourse is a kind of marriage. That's why God forbids a married man to have sex with a woman other than his wife. Adultery is a kind of multiple marriage. It seems that the main purpose of marriage is physical oneness: sex! Now, if that be true (and it is because Jesus said so), then premarital sex is saying that marriage is not important, only sexual oneness is important. Yet we know that is not true. In order for two people to experience total oneness, there must be real communication in three dimensions. Total oneness should follow this God-ordained pattern:

• Mental oneness
• Spiritual oneness
• Physical oneness

We all know how physical oneness is achieved: through sexual intercourse. However, what about the other two dimensions? What precedes and precludes sexual oneness? How are these unions achieved? They are the results of a very special friendship between two people who have really learned to communicate. In fact, it seems to me that the whole purpose of a dating relationship is to develop the kind of friendship in which a male and female become one in spirit, thought, emotion, and will. The dating relationship allows God to make two people one in every vital area of Christian fellowship. When spiritual oneness results, and two people find themselves in love, then marriage and the physical union are the celebration of that spiritual bond that exists. So, if you follow my reasoning, premarital sex is a reversal of God's order. It is saying that the purpose of dating is to achieve physical oneness. God says *no!* He says that's the purpose of marriage!

Sex, if it is to be God blessed and meaningful, must be the expression of spiritual oneness; it needs the security and commitment that marriage alone can give. A total marriage is made up of at least three foundations: spiritual oneness, social responsibility (a legal union), and physical oneness.

Reversing God's purpose often leads to severe problems in the love relationship. The couple that has premarital sex is saying that the physical relationship is more important than the spiritual relationship. They are in danger of neglecting their spiritual union and their communication as friends.

The Physical Versus the Spiritual

Making love and being in love are not always the same thing. When the relationship becomes physical before marriage, a girl tends to question if her guy really loves her for herself or just for her body. Evidence that this is true was discovered in a national collegiate survey. When asked why they had sex, only five percent of the men said they had sex because they loved the girl. Ninety-five percent of the men said they had sex for the pleasure of it or the curiosity of it. Surprisingly, the girls surveyed responded just the opposite. Ninety-five percent of the college women interviewed said they gave sex out of love; only five percent used sex for its physical pleasure alone.[3]

What all this tells us is that males and females have differing attitudes toward the use of our bodies. This imposes differing leadership roles during the dating relationship. Because the woman wants to please her man, she is tempted to give her body in response to his sexual aggressiveness. However, if she does give in, she then questions his leadership and motives. He in turn faces the problem of loss of respect for her. It is wise to really hear what your partner is saying when he or she says, "I love you." When a godly woman says, "I love you," what she means is, "I need you to protect me, lead me, help me show you the kind of tenderness that makes you a better man." You see, the woman's virtue inspires her man to spiritual leadership. One thing is sure: A man who cares for his woman wants to please her! If she sets her boundaries where her body is concerned, a godly man will honor those boundaries. When a godly man tells his girl, "I love you," what he means is, "I need your approval, your warmth, and your loyalty. I need you to inspire me to live up to my potential." Thus, the man may reach out for sex, but he really wants something else. He wants to know she really cares. She can raise his sights to noble male leadership. Putting the physical ahead of the spiritual can damage trust, and there can be no real love without trust.

Sex and the Mind

Ann Landers, in her syndicated newspaper column, made the statement that the great orgasm happens between the ears. The mind, she says, is where the fantasy of sexual bliss takes place. She is right. In his lecture to college students, called "Maximum Sex," Josh McDowell declares that the greatest sex organ is the brain. Sexual fulfillment is an attitude of the mind. Beauty is in the eye (or mind) of the beholder. What turns one person on sexually turns another off. This relates to premarital sex in a very definite way. God wants your mind to be free of lust, sensuality, and sexual perversion. He wants your mind to be pure. Then, when you fall in love and marry, the only experience you have will be with your wife or husband. Your fantasies of mind about sex will center around your mate.

What happens to the single person who has violated God's admonition to abstain from fornication? He runs the risk of bringing to his marriage bed many previous fantasies and experiences. The human mind is like a giant computer. It can retain 2 billion individual facts. It does not easily forget or erase previous information fed into it. Those who have had many sexual experiences with different sex partners, prior to marriage, run the risk of bringing all those experiences to their marriage beds. It's almost like bringing a crowd of old lovers into your bedroom! How awful and degrading! But it happens all the time to those who experienced sex throughout their single years. As a pastor and counselor, I've had numerous married men and women tell me how thoughts and fantasies of previous sex acts had come into their minds while they were trying to have a meaningful sex experience with their marriage partner.

Stolen Apples Taste Best

No wonder God wants us innocent on our wedding nights! Listen, Satan is no fool. He knows that stolen apples always seem to taste best. He'll see to it that any porno books you read and any dirty pictures you looked at come to mind. He'll try to make married sex seem tame and boring in comparison to illicit sex. He wants to make you dissatisfied with your wife or husband. And, like it or not, you give him permission to do it when you are loose with sex before marriage.

However, the couple who are virgins on their wedding night do not face this problem. They learn together. They build their fantasies together. Married sex is all they ever know, and therefore it's the best they'll ever know. Isn't God smart? He figured that out ages ago!

As if all this were not enough reason to wait till marriage, there are some other rather obvious practical reasons why any couple should wait:

- The danger of pregnancy is always present. There is no totally foolproof contraceptive. The most effective prevention is abstinence.
- It is poor Christian witness.
- The worry over an unexpected pregnancy and the possibility of being rushed into marriage are harmful to both persons.

A good sex life before marriage or during marriage is no guarantee of a happy love relationship. Waiting until marriage has more advantages than disadvantages. The main thing is to communicate. Love doesn't just happen; you must work at learning to give, building trust, and being dependable and loyal. Determine to become one in spirit. Let Christ's love bind your hearts together.

For Those Who Have Failed

What if you have already failed to hold the line sexually? Can you begin again? Yes, praise God, you can. Jesus begins with you at the place you begin with Him. He can forgive and cleanse us from all unrighteousness (1 John 1:9). He can erase the computer. You don't have to live with the guilt of past failures. You can be morally pure again.

Let me suggest some ABCs of overcoming guilt:

*A*dmit your sin to God. Confess it to Him.
*B*elieve Jesus can and will forgive you.
*C*ommit your sexual needs to Christ.
*D*o it daily. This is a war, not a battle.
*E*arnestly seek His will in your dating life.

Source Notes

1. "Fornication" is translated from the Greek word *pornia,* from which we get the English word *pornographic.* It describes sexual immorality among single people.
2. A Kinsey report shows that although women who had previous sex experience adjusted more quickly to their husbands, virgins soon caught up, and that 86 percent of the virgins achieved sexual

oneness after a year, when 85 percent of the nonvirgins did. Evelynn Millis Duvall, *Why Wait Till Marriage?* (NY: Association Press, 1965), p. 53.
3. *Readers Digest,* "How Men Really Feel About Sex and Love," January, 1978, pp. 83–86.

Additional Reading

Capper, W. Melville, and William, H. Morgan. *Toward Christian Marriage*. Downers Grove, IL: Inter-Varsity Press, 1958.

Duvall, Evelynn. *Love and the Facts of Life*. NY: Association Press, 1963.

Duvall, Evelynn. *Why Wait Till Marriage?* NY: Association Press, 1965.

Duvall, Evelynn, and Duvall, Sylvanus. *Sense and Nonsense About Sex*. NY: Association Press, 1962. *See* chapter five, "Love Is Not the Same as Sex," pp. 72–89.

Pemberton, Lois. *The Stork Didn't Bring You*. Nashville, TN: Thomas Nelson House, 1965.

Price, Eugenia. *Make Love Your Aim*. Grand Rapids, MI: Zondervan, 1972.

Public Affairs Committee. *Teen Love, Teen Marriage*. NY: Grosset & Dunlap, 1966.

Trobisch, Walter. *I Loved a Girl*. NY: Harper & Row, 1975.

Witt, Elmer N. *Life Can Be Sexual*. St. Louis, MO: Concordia Publishing, 1967.

11   *Can a Christian Date or Marry a Non-Christian?*

Can a Christian date or marry a non-Christian? Here are two questions rolled into one. They need to be answered together, because we usually marry someone we've dated. Have you noticed that? Can a Christian marry a non-Christian? Of course he can. There is no law against it that I know of! However, if a Christian wants a total Christian marriage, marrying an unbeliever is not the way to get there. Marrying a non-Christian is much like playing Russian roulette with a loaded pistol. The result can be devastating. We all know a Christian whose marriage partner is not a believer. That Christian settled for less than a total Christian marriage. He or she may love the spouse very much but will have to admit that much is missing in their relationship.

Where It All Begins

Someone has said you should only marry a best friend. Friendships are developed through dating. In fact, dating is a special kind of friendship. The marriage is usually no more successful than the dating relationship. How you relate as a couple, while dating, sets the pattern for how you will relate while you are married.

Because dating habits so vitally affect a marriage, it is important that we, as Christians, decide whom we will and will not date. Should you date an unbeliever? Well, before I get into that, we need to be reminded that you never know who you'll fall in love with—right? About the best you can do is eliminate some prospects by just not dating them. God's Word gives us some advice about dating and marriage.

111

Unequally Yoked

The Apostle Paul warned the Corinthian believers not to be ". . . unequally yoked together . . ." with unbelievers (2 Corinthians 6:14 KJV). The New American Standard Bible translates this phrase, "Do not be bound together . . . ." Paul had in mind being bound together sexually, as in a marriage relationship. He knew the pitfalls of such a union.

To avoid an unhappy marriage, one must determine to have a God-honoring date life. Dating is a kind of trial marriage. It's scouting the field for a prospective life partner. However, dating should be more than that. It should be the means to building valuable friendships. What are some purposes for dating?

- To develop your personality
- To develop you socially
- To overcome fear and shyness
- To cause you to grow in Christ
- To select a mate for life

All of these are valid reasons for dating. However, there is one very basic purpose for dating someone you think you might like to marry. The purpose for dating one person only is to unite the two of you spiritually. Exclusive dating relationships are to develop the deepest possible kind of friendship. It is a yoking together to see how much you have in common and how much you care about each other. Now, should a Christian develop an exclusive dating relationship with an unbeliever? I don't think he or she should. Let me explain why.

Being a Friend

Those who care enough about each other to establish an exclusive dating relationship should at least be close friends. What are the responsibilities that go along with being a close friend? [1] Two people are close friends only when they feel the freedom to discuss spiritual goals and feel the freedom to challenge each other to grow spiritually. If a Christian is dating an unbeliever, he must have the freedom to discuss spiritual things. What is the first spiritual goal for an unbeliever? Right—to become a believer! That was pretty obvious. Now, here's where the problem comes. To be in a dating relationship with an unbeliever is to be unequally yoked. The friendship is limited until the unbeliever comes to Christ. The Christian can only share the basics of how to be saved with the one he or she dates. If the dating partner receives Christ, then the friendship can deepen even further and the potential for an intimate spiritual friendship is there. However, what if the unbeliever refuses to be saved? What if he or she doesn't even want to talk about spiritual things? What does the Christian do now? Regretfully, it's often too late, especially if you are in love! Love is blind and naive many times, and we tend to think everything will work out after we're married. It seldom does. Marriage to a partner who does not know Christ is settling for so much less than God desires for His children. If two people aren't close enough friends to share spiritual oneness while dating, how can they think that marriage will unite their spirits? Marriage unites their bodies, not their souls. The purpose of dating is to develop that intimate friendship that comes from a common bond in Christ. The purpose of marriage is to unite two people physically. The physical union is to be the lifelong celebration of that deep spiritual union. This is God's plan for Christian marriage. Do you see why God says, "Be not unequally yoked"?

Total Marriage

God desires that Christian marriage be a total union. A total union includes a blending together of all we are. First Thessalonians 5:23 describes our personhood as ". . . spirit and soul and body . . . ." Total oneness must include fellowship between a man and woman on all three levels. Only those who are totally one in soul and spirit can experience the deepest oneness in sexual union. That's why Paul asks, ". . . what fellowship has light with darkness?" (2 Corinthians 6:14.) Well, what fellowship is there between a believer and a nonbeliever? A Christian can date a non-Christian, and they can share many "soulish" pleasures together: They may like the same things, share common ideas, and feel alike about various issues. However, when it comes down to issues that really matter such as: "Who am I?" "Why am I here?" "What is God's will for my life?" then it becomes clear that the believer and nonbeliever share no fellowship of the Spirit.

This is crucial. Without spiritual oneness the couple has no genuine basis for lasting communication or relationship. If two people are not united as to goals, ambitions, values, morals, and such, then what is there to hold them together? So you see, to date a nonbeliever becomes a self-defeating purpose. It is a dead-end street. Dating is a preparation for marriage, and marriage cannot be total without a spiritual bond.

Limited Marriage

How sad it is to see a courtship and then a marriage where the Christian partner cannot pray with his or her loved one. To be able to share everything except the most precious thing—the Lord Jesus—is a tragedy. The relationship is tragic because it is so limited. Dating and marriage should allow for growth. Love demands growth. If you love someone, you are committed to that person's character development. You desire to see that person become his or her best. If your loved one is lost, he will not let you develop his character. In fact, what often happens is that the believer is pulled away from Christ by the unbelieving partner. Then they are both in spiritual darkness!

Dating and Evangelism

The question is frequently raised in my dating seminars, "Why can't I date a lost person so that I can win him or her to Christ?" [2] You can, but beware of its pitfalls. Because God forbids you to marry an unbeliever, you must determine not to get romantically involved. This is not always easy to do. If you are mature enough to build a meaningful friendship with someone who is not a Christian, then there is the possibility God can use this friendship to share a witness for Christ. If a Christian is to date an unbeliever, let me suggest some guidelines.

- Establish from the beginning that there can be no romantic attachment or physical involvement.
- Determine to keep the relationship on a casual basis.

- Go only to Christian functions or in the company of other strong believers who can support you in your faith.
- Continually seek to involve your unsaved friend in spiritual discussions, readings, and activities.

However, even as I give these guidelines, I am aware of the heartaches that have come to so many who have fallen in love with the wrong person. God warns us to flee temptation before it ensnares us. Centuries ago Saint Augustine remarked that it is almost impossible to convince those in love that their love may not be God's will. Somehow those in love always think, "Love conquers all," or, "We'll work it out." If it doesn't work out to become a spiritual friendship during the dating relationship, it seldom ever does after marriage. Forewarned is forearmed!

Can a Christian date or marry a non-Christian? Not if he desires God's best for his life. Not if he wants total Christian marriage.

What Do I Do Now?

In our seminars I am frequently asked, "But I'm already married to an unbeliever; is there hope for me?" Paul gives us some guidance here. It's recorded in 1 Corinthians 7:10–16. The apostle tells the Christian not to leave the unbelieving mate, but to continue to try to win him or her to Christ. He says the believer can *sanctify* the unbeliever (1 Corinthians 7:14). This means God can use the Christian to reach the non-Christian.[3]

Often this is very difficult, and the Christian partner suffers great soul agony over the lost spouse. This is sad, but necessary, now that he or she is wed to the partner. Paul says, "For how do you know, O wife, whether you will save your husband? Or how do you know, O husband, whether you will save your wife?" (1 Corinthians 7:16.) You don't know! That's why it's best for those who are single not to get romantically involved with the lost. It can save much grief and heartache.

A final word of help is needed. Prayer is a powerful force for good. Our heavenly Father wants each home to glorify Him, so we know He hears the prayer of a saved partner praying for a lost mate. The believer needs to know how to pray for the lost. There is more to it than just saying, "God, save my lost husband. Amen." I suggest you read the chapter, "The ABC's of Praying for the Lost" in my book *Questions Non-Christians Ask*.[4] God honors the burdened soul of a marriage partner. He will hear and answer your prayers.

Source Notes

1. My Love/Life Principle Seminar notebook contains a detailed discussion of the responsibilities of friendships. See pp. 22–24.
2. I lead a dating seminar called Love/Life Principles for high-school and college-age youth. These seminars deal with friendships, dating, love, and sex.
3. Allan J. Peterson, *For Women Only* (Wheaton, IL: Tyndale House, 1974). See "Win Him to Christ," p. 144.
4. Barry Wood, *Questions Non-Christians Ask* (Old Tappan, NJ: Fleming H. Revell, 1977), pp. 145–153.

Additional Reading

Andrews, Gini. *Your Half of the Apple: God and the Single Girl.* Grand Rapids, MI: Zondervan, 1972.

Capper, W. Melville and William, H. Morgan. *Toward Christian Marriage.* Downers Grove: Inter-Varsity Press, 1958.

Small, Dwight H. *Design for Christian Marriage.* Old Tappan, NJ: Fleming H. Revell, 1959.

12 What Can I Believe About Baptism?

A college student prayed to receive Christ through the leadership of a Christian campus ministry. I met the young man a few weeks later and asked him about his decision to follow Christ. He gave an enthusiastic testimony of how Christ had saved him. I asked if he had given any thought to being baptized. His response was remarkable. He said, "Why, no, I haven't. Why should I be baptized? I'm already a Christian. Baptism is a church thing, isn't it?" His conclusion represents the thinking of many new believers who have found Christ outside the church. Water baptism just isn't important to some modern-day Christians. That's why this chapter is included in the book. When faced with the subject of water baptism, we face two temptations: to make too much of it or to make too little of it. Such extreme positions have caused much misunderstanding.

Differing Ideas

I know of no doctrine within the Church which is more divisive than baptism. There are as many ideas about it as there are denominations. A new Christian is often bewildered by all the differing opinions. One group practices infant baptism, another immerses in water, while another baptizes for salvation, and yet another rejects baptism altogether. What is the truth about baptism? What can we believe about it?

Scripture and Tradition

Much of the problem could be resolved if Christians could agree upon a common source of authority for doctrinal beliefs. Unfortunately, this is not the case. Historically, the Christian Church has held to at least two sources of authority: tradition and the Scriptures. Some groups use both church tradition and Scripture to determine their beliefs, while others may reject tradition altogether. This can lead to different conclusions, especially when tradition and Scripture do not agree. This helps us understand why there are so many ideas about baptism. Many practices regarding baptism have been handed down for centuries and have their source in Christian tradition rather than the Bible. Tradition and God's Word do not always agree. Yet, it needs to be said that not all traditions are bad either. There are some very good and valid Christian traditions that, even though they are not spelled out in Scripture, still support and affirm Scripture. For example, the New Testament does not directly affirm the practice of tithing as mandatory for a Christian. Yet, many churches have traditionally urged their people to practice tithing. This is a good tradition. Each believer must decide for himself the value he places upon tradition as it relates to God's Word. What we determine as our authority will reflect itself in our beliefs about baptism and other Christian doctrines.

Two Memorials
   In trying to decide what to believe about baptism, we can begin with the teaching of Jesus. Christ left the early church two symbolic memorials of His life and work: the Lord's Supper and baptism. Both of these are portraits of His saving work on the cross. They illustrate the life, death, burial, and resurrection of our Lord. The problem arises when we try to establish the purpose of these symbols. Historically churches have looked upon baptism two ways. Some see it as a sacrament (that is, a saving act or means of grace). Others view baptism as merely an ordinance, or memorial, having no saving effect. In order to decide what meaning we give to baptism, it will be necessary to study the Bible to search out its origins and meaning.

The Meaning of the Word
   The English word *baptize* comes from the Greek word *baptizo*. This word is from the older word *bapto,* which means to dip, dye, or

immerse. The verb *baptizo* is found seventy-four times in the New Testament. The word *baptism* is the transliteration of the Greek word *baptisma*. This noun is found twenty-two times in the New Testament and means "immersion," or "the act of immersing." [1]

A Roman Catholic authority recognizes that water baptism *formerly* was by immersion, not sprinkling. A good biblical reference to the meaning of the Greek word is found in the Septuagent (the Greek text of the Old Testament). This Greek Bible was much in use in Christ's day. He often quoted from it. In 2 Kings 5, we read the story of a pagan soldier, Naaman. This Syrian general was a leper. He came to Israel to be healed by the prophet Elisha. Elisha told Naaman to go to the river Jordan and there immerse himself seven times, and then he would be healed. The King James version says Elisha told him to *dip* himself. The New American Standard says he told him to *wash* himself. Now, the Greek word used here is the verb *baptizo* (2 Kings 5:10). Verse 14 of the New American Standard Bible says Naaman *dipped* himself seven times. The same Greek verb is used again. The point is very clear. The word *baptizo* means "I bury," "I submerge," "I dunk," or "I immerse." That's what Naaman did. Here the word is used in its natural sense, not in the context of baptism.

The Message of Baptism

Now to the questions, "Does baptism in water wash away sins?" "Is baptism necessary to salvation?" Scripture makes it very clear that only the sacrifice of the blood of Jesus can wash away sin (Ephesians 1:7; Hebrews 7:26, 27). Scripture does not uphold the idea that baptism is a sacrament (a saving act). Scripture rather asserts that baptism is a symbol, a memorial portraying salvation.

Who Is Qualified to Be Baptized?

The answer is: only a born-again child of God. Scripture teaches only believer's baptism. It is for those who are already saved. In Acts 8:36, 37 the African from Ethiopia asked Phillip, "What prevents me from being baptized?" To which Phillip replied, " '. . . If you believe with all your heart you may.' And he answered and said, '. . . I believe that Jesus Christ is the Son of God.' " The condition for his immersion was his faith in Jesus. His faith saved him, not baptism. This is also revealed in Acts 10, when Peter comes to the house of the Roman centurion, Cornelius. Cornelius and others of his household had already been converted and had received the Holy Spirit before they were baptized. Peter asked the skeptical Jewish delegation, "Surely no one can refuse the water for these to be baptized who have received the Holy Spirit just as we did, can he?" (Acts 10:47.) Notice, they had already received the Holy Spirit and had not yet been baptized. Salvation preceded the symbol of salvation.

Why Should Believers Be Baptized?

Water baptism is the new Christian's first act of obedience to Jesus. Jesus commanded His disciples, "Go therefore and make disciples of all the nations, baptizing them in the name of the Father and the Son and the Holy Spirit" (Matthew 28:19). Since baptism of believers is commanded by Christ, it imposes upon the believer a responsibility to obey Christ.

The New Testament teaches that the command to be baptized should be obeyed by the new Christian as soon as possible after conversion. If you are saved and know it, be baptized to show it! In Philippi, the Apostle Paul baptized the jailer who was converted that very night (Acts 16:33). At Pentecost Peter and the disciples baptized those who believed that same day (Acts 2:41). Paul was baptized three days after his own conversion (Acts 9:18).

What Is God's Purpose in Baptism?

Baptism is God's object lesson to the world. It illustrates the Gospel story—the cross and resurrection. It is God's first-century method of audiovisual education. The believer pantomimes the Gospel story: ". . . Christ died for our sins according to the Scriptures, and that He was buried, and that He was raised on the third day according to the Scriptures" (1 Corinthians 15:3, 4). This is to be continued by every believer until Christ comes to earth again.

What Should I Do?

Suppose you are a new Christian, and as yet you have not been baptized as a public witness of your salvation. What should you do?

I can understand this dilemma, because I've been there. I did not personally receive Christ until I was a teenager, yet I had been educated in church schools and had been a "religious" child. After being saved, the question of baptism arose. Someone asked me when I was going to be baptized. A bit surprised, I replied that I had been baptized as a child. He then sought to explain to me that baptism was to follow, not precede, receiving Christ. At that point I was faced with a decision. This is true of many new Christians today. This can be a very valuable decision, because it forces us to study our Bibles and ask some very important questions about what we believe and why.

Heaven Is Not the Issue

It needs to be stated here very directly that whether or not a person is baptized has nothing whatsoever to do with one's eternal salvation. That was settled by the Lord Jesus on the cross. The moment one accepts Christ, God accepts him! The repentant thief beside Jesus at Golgotha believed and was saved. So it is with millions of true Christians who have not been baptized since receiving Christ. The issue is not salvation, but obedience. It seems clear that if a person understands God's Word on this issue, then he or she would want to please the Father by being scripturally baptized. Those in the Body of Christ who have not experienced the thrill of being symbolically buried and raised again with the Lord Jesus have missed a great blessing. May God use this Scripture study to help you and others plainly see God's teaching here.

Source Notes

1. Alan Richardson. *A Theological Word Book of the Bible* (NY: Macmillan, 1950), pp. 27–30. This volume contains a thorough discussion of the Old Testament and New Testament word usages and their meanings.
2. Henry M. Morris. *The Bible Has the Answer* (Nutley, NJ: Presbyterian and Reformed Pub. Co., 1971). See pp. 140–43 for Dr. Morris' survey of major denominations' ideas about the meaning and importance of water baptism.

13 *Does God Want Every Christian to Speak in Tongues?*

Does God want every believer to speak in tongues? Here's a question for which multitudes need an answer. This question has been very personal to me, at times, as I've tried to find Holy Spirit power in my life and ministry. Years ago, as a young evangelist, I became hungry for more of God's Spirit than I was experiencing. About this time I read a very provocative book, *They Speak With Other Tongues,* by John L. Sherrill.[1] This book shook me to the core! Mr. Sherrill was a reporter who investigated the tongues phenomenon and came away a believer and a participant. After having read his book, the question haunted me: "Barry, is that what's missing in your life?" That book and others like it started me on a search for the truth about this mysterious baptism of the Holy Spirit.

The Second Blessing

I have always been an avid reader of Christian biographies. I especially enjoy reading the lives of great preachers of the past. Men such as D. L. Moody, R. A. Torrey, C. H. Spurgeon, and many others have challenged and blessed my life. Frequently in my reading I came across statements by these men wherein they, too, were distressed by a feeling of barrenness and longed for an anointing, or empowering, of the Holy Spirit beyond anything they had known since conversion. Sometimes they testified to experiencing a second blessing of the Holy Spirit. Fifteen years ago I first read Andrew Murray's *The Full Blessing of Pentecost,*[2] in which this great man of God urged believers to seek the second blessing.

Confusion Upon Confusion

Every Christian is open to confusion if he listens to too many voices, especially when he makes the mistake of thinking that his experience with the Holy Spirit must be like everyone else's. This was my mistake. I was a young Christian looking too much toward experiences rather than to the Scriptures.

During this time of seeking, I actually sought the gift of tongues as the outward evidence that I had received the baptism of the Holy Spirit. The end result was more confusion. No doubt some would say I failed to get the gift because of my doubting unbelief or some unconfessed sin. Yet that is not true. What all this did accomplish was to cause me to put away all my books except the Book. Only as I prayerfully studied the Scriptures did I begin to sort out the biblical truths. Hopefully I can share some of those findings in these pages.

Our Great Need

Let us begin by confessing our great need as contemporary Christians. The church today, in most parts of the world, is destitute of Holy Spirit power. The church, corporately and individually is much like Samson of old, who shook himself and knew not that the power of the Lord was not upon him. Delilah's scissors of worldliness have cut off our Holy Spirit anointing. Many thousands of believers are disgusted with the institutional church which operates only from human resources. They hunger for a supernatural God, living through a supernatural church. However, in our search for renewal and renewed pentecostal power, there are some dangers. In our hunger and thirst for the fullness of the Spirit, we need to keep some principles in mind.

John R. W. Stott, in the opening pages of his wonderful book *The Baptism and Fullness of the Holy Spirit* [3] offers us three guidelines. First, he suggests we center our desire for the fullness of the Spirit in Scripture, not in the experience of some other individual or group. This is the lesson I had to learn. He says, ". . . we should neither covet for ourselves what God may have given to others, nor urge upon others what God may have given to us, unless it is plainly revealed in His Word that this is part of the inheritance promised to all his people.''

Second, as we search the Scriptures regarding any biblical doctrine, we should seek the truth in the didactic, or teaching, portions,
rather than the historical portions of Scripture. The importance of
this principle cannot be overstated. Too often those who teach about
tongues draw their scriptural examples from the narrative portions
of Acts, rather than the teachings of Jesus and the apostles. Dr. Stott
comments: "What is *described* in scripture as having happened to
others is not necessarily intended for us, whereas what is *promised*
to us we are to appropriate, and what is *commanded* us we are to
obey." [4] This is sound counsel. What he is saying is that we are to
base our doctrine of the Holy Spirit not on the apostles' experiences
but, rather, on the apostles' teachings. The apostles raised people
from the dead, but that does not mean that this is normative
behavior for the church today. Much of what we read in Acts of the
apostles was for a sign. Many miracles and events were proofs of the
risen Christ returning to His people in the person of the Holy Spirit.
Many of the events in their detail were temporary, local, and non-
repetitive. Pentecost and the coming of the Holy Spirit is a good
example. [5]

Third, in asking the question, "Does God want every Christian to
speak in tongues?" we should keep in mind that our motive is practical and personal, not academic or controversial. This has been my
motive throughout this book. As Dr. Stott again says, "We are
brethren. We love one another." It is not our purpose to attack any
group or to defend a theological dogma. Our purpose is to shed light,
not generate heat!

From Here Where?

Now, with these thoughts and principles behind us as a foundation, how do we begin to sort out the cloud of confusion that sur-
rounds the subject of speaking in tongues and the baptism of the
Holy Spirit?

My personal difficulty as an author centers around the problem
of being too technical and academic. This book is written for
the layman, not the theologian. Yet this question requires a serious
look at the Scriptures, because so many have let their feelings over-

ride the clear teachings of God's Word. Therefore, it is best to begin by defining some frequently used terms.

CHARISMATIC. Are you a charismatic? I've been asked that question many times over the last ten years. It seems evangelical Christianity is being divided into two camps today: charismatic and noncharismatic. This is unfortunate. Worse than that, it is of the devil! The Holy Spirit is the author of unity, not division (Ephesians 4:3, 4). Anything that divides Christ's body is not of God. The one area in which the church should be united is that of Holy Spirit fellowship. However, this is not the case. Well, *am* I charismatic? Are you? I only know one way to respond to that question. "Yes, I am a charismatic Christian, if you mean by that what Scripture means. However, if you mean have I received a second baptism of the Holy Spirit which has been evidenced by speaking in tongues, then the answer is, currently, no!" Let's examine this term *charismatic*. The word comes from a Greek New Testament word *charismata*. This word is used only twice in the New Testament: in 1 Corinthians 12:4 and Romans 12:6. It is a plural of the word *charis* meaning "grace," which is used of God's love for us. Thus *charismatic* is a transliteration of the Greek plural noun *charismata*. It literally means "graces," or a gift, or gifts, freely given. Now, speaking of spiritual (grace) gifts, Paul says, "But to each one is given the manifestation of the Spirit for the common good" (1 Corinthians 12:7). What does the apostle mean by this statement? What he is saying is that every Christian has been made charismatic, or grace gifted. Let me elaborate. At the moment one receives Christ, he is indwelt by the Holy Spirit. I dealt with this in detail in the chapter "Are All Church Members Born Again?" Every believer has the Holy Spirit living in him (Romans 8:9; Galatians 4:6). Someone has said that when the Holy Spirit comes into your heart, it's your birthday. The angels rejoice, and the Holy Spirit comes bearing gifts for your birthday. These are grace gifts or *charismata*. This grace gift is the "manifestation of the Spirit" Paul speaks of in 1 Corinthians. Thus, at salvation every believer was gifted. This gift (or gifts) is equipment to serve Christ through the church, ". . . for the common good." [6]

"It must be pointed out, however, that the Bible teaches that every Christian is truly charismatic. Every Christian has at least one gift sovereignly bestowed by the Holy Spirit as a personal spiritual birthright.'' [7]

BEING CHARISMATIC AND TONGUES. While we can say every believer is charismatic (grace gifted), that does not mean that every believer has received the same gift. It certainly does not mean we all have the grace of speaking in tongues. This matter of spiritual gifts needs to be understood by every Christian. For many years it was a neglected area of New Testament teaching. We all owe a great debt to what some call the "charismatic movement," because it has caused Bible teachers to take a renewed look at the importance of spiritual gifts. I grew up, as a Christian, never having heard of spiritual gifts, except an occasional slur from the pulpit against Pentecostals and speaking in tongues. I grew up thinking there was only one gift, and it was bad!

What Are Spiritual Gifts?

A brief word about these grace gifts is needed. There are many excellent books available on this subject, and I've listed some at the end of this chapter. I'll only give a general statement about the gifts. Yet, many new Christians know little or nothing about what God has given them. They are like a child at his own birthday party, staring in bewilderment at unopened presents, wondering what they contain. Okay, let's unwrap your gifts and see what they are! [8]

  • *They are spiritual gifts.* Gifts are not human talents, although a gift may be evidenced through a human talent. By definition, a spiritual gift is a supernatural grace endowment that the Holy Spirit gives the believer at the moment of his new birth, to enable the believer to perform spiritual ministry. Your gift is an ability of Christ in you to use for others. This is a very exacting truth to learn! Every new Christian is faced with the problem of trying to live like Jesus Christ. It is an impossible task! Yet Christ has come to live in us, and He has given each of us one or more of His own personality traits or abilities. For example, one of my gifts is that of a teacher of the Word. It thrills me to know that Christ, the Master Teacher, lives in me and has graced me with His teaching abilities. Therefore Christ Himself can minister His teaching ministry through me. That's exciting! Every believer has divine enablement for ministry.

• *They are sovereign gifts.* You and I have the gift, or gifts, God wants us to have, not the gifts *we* want. Paul says, "But one and the same Spirit works all these things, distributing to each one individually just as He wills" (1 Corinthians 12:11). He says the same thing in verse eighteen. God gave you the gift He wanted you to have. It was given at your spiritual birthday. Spiritual gifts are salvation gifts, and they are sovereign; God decides, not us. This can be very helpful when we understand its implications. You see, you don't have to seek someone else's gift. You don't have to seek *any* gift. You already have exactly what God wants you to have. Paul tells Timothy to stir up the gift that is within him (2 Timothy 1:6). Paul tells the Corinthians to *cultivate* the best gifts.[9] Because this is true, if God wants us to speak in an unknown tongue, or receive a prayer language as some call it, then we do not have to ask for it or have someone lay hands on us to receive it. If God wants us to speak in tongues, then faith is the key, not seeking or asking. It is dangerous to start praying outside the will of God. Someone other than God may answer that prayer. If Satan cannot defeat us, he'll deceive us. Some tongues are Satanic. I have known people who received a demonic tongue by seeking after a tongues experience. Please do not misread my meaning here. Not all tongues are Satanic. There is a place in today's church for scriptural tongues. However, they are sovereignly bestowed, and we are not to seek them.

• *They are service gifts.* Scripture says the gifts have a different purpose. They are ". . . for the common good" (1 Corinthians 12:7). They are for ministry (1 Peter 4:10).

Spiritual gifts are given to the individual believer to equip him to be a servant. Your gift is for me; my gift is for you. We are to use our gifts to build up the body of Christ (Ephesians 4:11, 12). What this means is that gifts are not for personal use, but for public use. Paul stresses this very point about the gift of tongues. In 1 Corinthians 14, he makes this very clear in the first twenty verses. He explains, ". . . one who prophesies speaks to men for edification and exhortation and consolation. One who speaks in a tongue edifies himself; but one who prophesies edifies the church" (1 Corinthians 14:3, 4). Because the gift of tongues is very limited in its service to the church, Paul relegates it to a place of lesser importance than preaching (prophecy). Therefore, we are not to seek any gift for selfish or personal reasons. They are for service.

Are Tongues for Us Today?

Having learned some basic facts about these marvelous grace gifts, it's now time to examine the phenomenon of speaking in an unknown tongue. Is this experience real? Is it valid for today's church? The church is often divided on this subject. One of the reasons for the division is a lack of understanding. Often those who are called charismatic are misrepresented by those who are not. One group claims the full Gospel, while the other claims the true Gospel. As I've observed Christian groups through the years, it's obvious that we frequently go to extremes in doctrine and practice. A pastor friend of mine, Dr. Bill Bennett, of Fort Smith, Arkansas, observed that those who cause the tongues fuss can be described as extremists. There are those who have *charisphobia*. I agree with him. *Charismania* describes those who have made speaking in tongues an obsession. *Charisphobia* is the other extreme; it is an unusual fear of tongues, as though this gift were a time bomb rather than a gift. The answer is not in charismania or charisphobia; the biblical truth is found in the charismata of tongues. It behooves us to focus our attention on what the Scriptures really say about tongues, not on what some contemporary group portrays tongues to be.

Scriptural Tongues

The first truth I see in Scripture is that tongues *are* a gift. Paul himself could say, "I thank God, I speak in tongues more than you all" (1 Corinthians 14:18). Not only that, but the apostle said, ". . . I wish that you all spoke in tongues" (1 Corinthians 14:5). The question arises as to whether or not these words are addressed only to the Corinthians or whether they have application for all believers in all ages. Admittedly, Bible students are divided on this. For the present I want us to assume that tongues are a legitimate gift operating in the church today. I personally feel this is the correct approach to Scripture. However, we will examine the possibility that tongues ceased in the first century and are not operational today. We will forgo that study momentarily.

PSYCHIC TONGUES. Even as we state that there are authentic scriptural tongues operating in the church today, it needs to be said that not all tongues-speaking today is genuine. Not all tongues-speaking is of God. Within the Neo-Pentecostal movement there exists what some have termed "psychic" or "psychological" tongues-speaking. This is a learned, self-induced, emotional, conditional, willed tongue. This happens when a person hears others speaking in their prayer language, as it is called, and then is encouraged to receive this gift also. This receiving the gift of tongues is accompanied by coaching and instruction, in which one is told how to free his mind and loosen his tongue. He starts saying *hallelujah* as fast as he can and starts speaking in tongues. This kind of activity is a part of that charismania we were talking about. This is not scriptural tongues and has done much harm to many people.

SATANIC TONGUES. Another nonscriptural experience with unknown tongues is direct Satanic tongues-speaking. This is much like psychic tongues (which is in reality inspired of the devil), only in this case such a gift is directly of Satan. What is a Satanic tongue? It is a previously unlearned language that comes forth from a person's mouth, which has its source from a demon spirit living within that person. It is a demon speaking, using the vocal apparatus of the person he indwells. This sounds strange and unbelievable to those who have no acquaintance with such matters, but it is true nonetheless. Demonic tongues can be offered in a church service, giving every appearance of glorifying God; but in reality, if we knew what was really being said, we would be shocked at the blasphemies coming forth. Two real evidences of Satan-inspired tongues are confusion over tongues in the church and a glorifying of the flesh.

Are Tongues for a Sign?

Because Satan has done so much deception in the area of tongues-speaking, there are many Bible teachers who fail to see any authentic purpose for tongues today. Such reasoning states that tongues were "for a sign" in the early church and then ceased with the writing of the Scriptures and the passing away of the apostles. Those who teach this see all the miraculous gifts listed in 1 Corinthians 12:9, 10 as sign gifts. These include the gift of miracles, healing, tongues, and interpretation of tongues. It is said that these gifts were temporary and used by the Holy Spirit, through the apostles, as proofs or signs of Christ's resurrection power. When the Scriptures were written (the New Testament) there was no more need of these gifts, and they disappeared from the church. Therefore, if one follows this teaching, there are no authentic scriptural tongues today, and God certainly has no place for these in the church. The only conclusion to draw from this is that all modern tongues are fraudulent.

Tongues Then Shall Cease

How does one arrive at this position? There are some very capable theologians who advocate this position, and yet I can't agree with them. Such teaching is based upon Paul's words in 1 Corinthians 13:8–10 (KJV):

> Charity never faileth: but whether there be prophecies, they shall fail; whether there be tongues, they shall cease; whether there be knowledge, it shall vanish away. For we know in part, and we prophesy in part. But when that which is perfect is come, then that which is in part shall be done away.

Notice the phrase ". . . whether there be tongues, they shall cease . . . ." It is argued that this verb *cease* in the original is in what grammarians call the middle voice, which can be translated "shall of themselves cease." Thus, it is explained that Paul's meaning is that tongues shall gradually, of themselves, cease to be a part of God's gifts to the church. It is further argued that ". . . when that which is perfect is come . . ." is Paul's reference to the writing of the New Testament. So we are told tongues will, of themselves, cease with the writing of the New Testament and the death of the apostles.

Another Explanation
There are some problems with this explanation. It is always questionable to take a theological position based on only one passage of Scripture, which is what some have done who reject modern tongues altogether. Their only proof is this explanation of 1 Corinthians 13:8–10. This is particularly faulty when there is another explanation of the same verses which gives the opposite meaning! Paul's use of the middle voice could have been his way of affirming the continuation of tongues until Jesus returns at the end of the age. To amplify this, let's ask two questions. First, does the middle voice of *to cease* always imply the idea "of themselves"? [10] Second, does the phrase, ". . . when that which is perfect is come . . ." have to mean when the Scriptures were written? My response to both of these questions is *no*. First of all, Paul could have used the middle voice for emphasis. This use of the middle voice puts emphasis on the subject of the verb. Used this way, it would translate "if there are tongues, even they shall cease." Paul's meaning would then be that even tongues, which the Corinthian church made so much of, would eventually cease to be used. They would not pass away of themselves, but even tongues, like prophecy, would cease to be needed. Now to the second question. The phrase ". . . when the perfect is come . . ." could refer to the Second Coming of Christ, not the writing of the New Testament. Indeed that is Paul's meaning. He refers to the completion of all things, "For now we see in a mirror dimly, but then face to face . . ." (1 Corinthians 13:12). I fail to see how these words can refer to the New Testament. Paul's meaning

probably is the return of Christ. This interpretation solves the problem in verse eight about prophecies ceasing along with tongues. Those who say the sign gifts ended with the apostolic age must explain why preaching (prophecy) continues.[11] Paul's meaning is much more easily understood when we consider that all the gifts will cease at the return of Christ.

Tongues Are for a Sign

Please forgive this technical, detailed explanation, but it is necessary in order to arrive at solid biblical understanding. I've taken time to observe that tongues are not for a sign, in the sense of being temporary or apostolic only. However, the Scriptures do say tongues are for a sign. First Corinthians 14:22 says tongues are a sign to unbelievers. Paul is saying that tongues are a supernatural enablement so that when the Gospel is preached, unbelievers will hear and understand that God has spoken. Tongues then are a miracle of translation or a miracle of hearing or both. Tongues then are primarily for evangelism, as was the case at Pentecost in Acts 2. This is the only place in Scripture in which tongues are said to be for a sign.

Tongues and the Baptism of the Holy Spirit

Now we come to a hairy issue. Are tongues a sign of the baptism of the Holy Spirit? No, they are not. However, we are often asked, "Have you received the baptism of the Holy Ghost?" which means, "Have you received a second, deeper work of the Holy Spirit after conversion, which is evidenced by speaking in tongues?" It's time we laid this kind of wording to rest, never to resurrect it again. While it may be valid for a modern Christian to have the grace gift of tongues, it is not valid to call it the baptism of the Holy Spirit and to seek it as a second work of grace.

As already stated, 1 Corinthians 14:22 is the only reference to tongues as a sign. They are for evangelism. This is exactly what we find in Scripture.

- *Acts 2—the Jewish Pentecost.* Here tongues were manifested for evangelistic purposes. They were a sign to unbelievers.

- *Acts 10—Peter goes to Cornelius.* Here Gentiles were saved and spoke in tongues. In this instance tongues were a sign of salvation, not a subsequent second baptism of the Spirit. This Gentile Pentecost was their baptism in the Spirit (salvation).
- *Acts 19—Paul at Ephesus.* Here Paul met a group of people who had heard of Jesus through the preaching of Apollos. They were called disciples but had not been born again. They were like Old Testament believers. Their knowledge of the way of salvation was incomplete. Paul preached to them. They received the truth and were saved. As evidence of this Spirit baptism, they were baptized in water, and tongues were given as evidence of their full salvation. This was another Gentile Pentecost on the mission field.

This Is Not a Second Blessing

These tongues experiences in Acts (that's all there are) which we have cited all have one thing in common! They agree with 1 Corinthians 14:22. Tongues were not given as a second blessing or baptism of the Spirit to a believer. Tongues were a salvation gift, given as a sign of salvation. It is never correct to call a second, deepening work of the Holy Spirit the baptism of the Spirit. The New Testament knows no such language. The only time Scripture speaks of Spirit baptism, it is describing salvation (the new birth)! The baptism of the Spirit has nothing to do with tongues or any other gift. It is the initial Christian experience. It is synonymous with the gift of the Holy Spirit received at conversion. Dr. John R. W. Stott says, "The 'baptism' of the spirit is a universal Christian experience because it is the initial Christian experience. This is the general teaching of the New Testament." [12] It is further noted that, of the seven times the baptism of the Spirit is spoken of in the New Testament, each has to do with the initial experience of salvation. Dr. Stott summarizes by saying: "It is difficult to resist the conclusion that the baptism of the Spirit is not a second and subsequent experience, enjoyed by some Christians, but the initial experience enjoyed by all." [13]

Is There a Second Blessing?

What are we to think of all this talk of a second blessing? Once you can get it out of your head that speaking in tongues is the second blessing received after salvation, then it's possible to understand what God's Word does say about Christian growth. Scripture speaks of the fullness of the Spirit in our lives. We are told to be daily filled with God's Spirit (Ephesians 5:18). This fullness is nothing less than letting Christ's Spirit control us. Some Christians do experience a crisis, years after conversion, that brings them to a renewed and deeper experience with God. They then enter into this fullness of the Spirit. Yet it is not automatic or continual, unless accompanied by faith and obedience. This fullness does not have to come as a crisis. We can grow in this fullness from the day of salvation. Some preachers, laymen, and others have received from the Father a special anointing of the Spirit for ministry. This has been called a baptism by some, but this is incorrect language! It is an anointing for service. You could say Billy Graham has a special anointing for world-wide evangelism.

Tongues Are Not the Blessing

What I want to make clear is that receiving tongues, or any other gift, will not make a believer a better Christian. Remember, the gifts of the Spirit are for service and ministry. They have nothing whatever to do with Christian conduct or character. Holiness does not come from the gifts; it comes from the Giver! Therefore do not seek a gift to make you holier. Gifts are for service, not sanctification. Seek the fullness of the Spirit. It will make you like Jesus.

What Are Tongues, Anyway?

Whenever someone asks, "Do you have the baptism?" what are they really asking? Regardless of the terminology used, we need to understand what is being said. The modern charismatic movement is known for teaching others to speak in tongues. It's now time to examine just what this means. Most often those who speak of the gift of tongues are referring to what charismatics call the prayer language. This consists of praying in unintelligible syllables, or sounds, which are termed a heavenly language of the Spirit. Those who use their prayer language testify to having a great joy in the Lord. Their prayer language helps them praise God and intercede for others. It is such a great experience that many who have it want you to have it, too.

THE PRAYER LANGUAGE AND SCRIPTURE. How are we to react to those who want everyone to experience the prayer language or a tongue? I find it helpful to point out some very interesting things in the New Testament about the gift of tongues. The problem is that those who feel everyone should have this gift are always using the Book of Acts as the proof text. They point out that those people in Acts spoke in tongues, some after they were saved. As we've seen, this just was not the case. However, there is a greater problem. It is not easy to conclude that the gift of tongues in Acts is the same as what people call the prayer language today. We are told that the prayer language is the language of angels spoken of in 1 Corinthians 13:1. If that's true, this gift of tongues in Acts is different. Let's just compare tongues in Acts and tongues in Corinth.

Tongues in Acts	*Tongues in Corinth*
• They are a foreign language heard and known on earth (Acts 2).	• They are a heavenly language not known or understood or both (1 Corinthians 14:14; 18:1).
• There was no interpretation needed (Acts 2; 10; 19).	• There must be an interpretation (1 Corinthians 14:27, 28).
• Their purpose was evangelism as a sign of Acts 1:8.	• Their purpose is self-edification (1 Corinthians 14:4; 12:17).
• They were spoken to men, not God (Acts 2).	• They are spoken to God, not men (1 Corinthians 14:2, 28).

It is obvious, by observing the differences listed above, that tongues in Acts and tongues in Corinth are not the same thing. If however, a person does not accept these differences and says that tongues in Acts and Corinth are the same, then another conclusion must also be drawn.

MODERN TONGUES A FOREIGN LANGUAGE. If all tongues in the New Testament are the same, then all modern tongues must be known languages on earth, not angelic, heavenly prayer languages. Why is this conclusion true? Because the only place in Scripture where tongues are clearly defined is in Acts 2. Here they are foreign languages heard by unbelievers. They are known tongues, not tongues unknown to the hearers. In Corinth we are not clearly told what tongues are. We must infer that they are prayer languages. This then leads us to say that, because they are different, Acts cannot be used as a proof text for seeking to receive a prayer language.

FOR WHAT IT'S WORTH. My own understanding of tongues is that tongues in Acts and Corinth are indeed different, but that both can be active today. Tongues may be manifested as a foreign language spoken for the lost to understand. They would be accompanied by either an interpretation by another person other than the tongue spoken or by the miracle of hearing, as at Pentecost. The gift of tongues may be manifested as a private prayer language spoken to God, with the result of self-edification. Tongues may even be ecstatic utterances with prophetic messages, needing an interpreter as a proof that God has spoken; then they are a sign to unbelievers.

HOW DO I GET IT? Finally, does God want every believer to speak in tongues? Obviously, He does not, no more than He wants every believer to have all the other gifts. He does want us to use the salvation gifts we do have. If He gifted you and me with tongues, we do not have to seek them, only be open to them. We are told in 1 Thessalonians 5:19, "Do not quench the Spirit." Paul says in 1 Corinthians 14:39, ". . . do not forbid to speak in tongues." This is wise counsel. We do not have to seek tongues or any other gift; we must only be open to God's leading and be submissive to His will. Because the gift of tongues is a secondary gift, limited in edification and service to the church, this gift need not occupy our minds and thoughts. There is a scriptural place for the gift of tongues, but it should not be an exalted gift.

Source Notes

1. John L. Sherrill, *They Speak With Other Tongues* (NY: McGraw-Hill, 1964).
2. Andrew Murray, *The Full Blessing of Pentecost* (Fort Washington, PA: Christian Literature Crusade, 1954).
3. John R. W. Stott, *The Baptism and Fullness of the Holy Spirit* (Downers Grove, IL: Inter-Varsity Press, 1964), pp. 8, 9.
4. Ibid., p. 9.
5. It should be observed that Pentecost was repeated three times: in Acts 2, at Jerusalem; in Acts 10, at Caesarea; and in Acts 19, at Ephesus. This repetition is to fulfill the promise of Acts 1:8 that the disciples would be witnesses in Jerusalem, Judea, Samaria, and the uttermost parts of the earth. This witness was in response to the coming of the Holy Spirit in power at the Jewish Pentecost, then at two Gentile pentecostal experiences.
6. There is a question among some as to whether or not a believer can have more than one gift of the Spirit. I believe he can. Bill Gothard, in his Institute in Basic Youth Conflicts, teaches otherwise.
7. David Shibley, *A Charismatic Truce* (Nashville, TN: Thomas Nelson, 1978), p. 18.
8. What is said about gifts in general is true of tongues in particular. Thus, in understanding principles about gifts, we shed light on the specific gift of tongues.
9. In 1 Corinthians 12:31, the verb *be jealous for* is translated by Dr. C. B. Williams in his New Testament as "cultivate," which captures the idea of this Greek verb.
10. For those who want a technical explanation, *of themselves* indicates what is called a reflexive middle. The middle voice can also be used to intensify the subject doing the action of the verb. This is the intensive middle.
11. A rather weak explanation has been offered. It is stated that prophecy, in the sense of foretelling the future, has ceased; and knowledge has ceased, in the sense of discerning knowledge of unlearned or future events. Yet neither of these statements is true. Prophecy and fulfillment have not ceased.

12. John R. W. Stott, *The Baptism and Fullness of the Holy Spirit* (Downers Grove, IL: Inter-Varsity Press, 1964), p. 21.
13. Ibid., p. 23.

Additional Reading

Stott, John R. W. *The Baptism and Fullness of the Holy Spirit.* Downers Grove, IL: Inter-Varsity Press, 1964. This is an excellent book.

14 Does the Bible Teach Evolution?

Every modern Christian faces the challenge of the credibility of the Bible. Christian students in a scientific environment are frequently faced with the challenge of evolution as an explanation of origins. Evolutionary theory says the earth was created in millions of years, whereas Genesis 1 says it only took God six days to create the earth. Obviously there is a conflict.

Many people show no concern over this issue and see it as peripheral. What is commonly stressed is that God exists and did the creating, and we should leave *how* He did it up to science. Many well-meaning Christians see evolution as God's "method of creation." In this kind of reasoning, evolution and Genesis have been wed together, and there is no conflict.

However, before one can wed this odd couple, some real concessions have to be made to evolution. To begin with, Genesis 1 must be viewed as merely poetry, allegory, or religious myth, before evolution and the Bible can coexist. Those who believe in evolution as *the* explanation of origins must of necessity soften and idealize the teachings of Genesis.

A Vital Issue

This chapter is written because untold numbers of young people, as well as adults, have had their faith in Scripture ravaged by evolutionary philosophy. This issue is not peripheral; it touches the very heart of our faith. Dr. Henry Morris has said:

139

Probably the most important single issue confronting
Biblical Christianity in these days is the question of origins.
The remaining strongholds of virile, Bible-centered Christian witness in the world seem everywhere to be in imminent
and serious danger of capitulation to the forces of
philosophical evolution . . . . For what a man believes
about ultimate origins and about God's revelation concerning creation will inevitably affect his beliefs concerning
destinies and purposes. The issue of evolution versus Biblical creation is most emphatically *not* a peripheral question.[1]

What Dr. Morris has said is that, unless we know where we came
from, we cannot know who we are and where we are going. The
Christian who tries to make evolutionary philosophy compatible
with biblical philosophy can only come out confused and weakened
as a believer. It is my contention that Scripture and evolution are
antithetical and diametrically opposed. Charles Darwin and King
James are not friends. They do not share the same world view, nor
do they teach the same thing. So, in answer to this question about
the Bible and evolution, let's begin by defining some terms.

What Is Evolution?
Webster's Dictionary defines the word *evolution* as an "unroll-
ing." It comes from the Latin word *evolutio.* A biology teacher in a
high-school classroom recently told her students that *evolution* only
means "change." She said *evolution* is a term which describes any
kind of biological or physical change in living organisms. Granted, if
that's all evolutionary theory teaches, then no Christian need see a
conflict between the Scriptures and biological evolution. All of us
can observe this horizontal change everywhere. A baby grows into
an adult; that is change. A seed grows into a plant; that is change.
Through hybrid breeding, change takes place within a given species
to create new varieties. This is observable every day. In fact, Scripture affirms this truth very clearly. Genesis 1 tells us that God
created everything after its kind (Genesis 1:11, 12, 21, 24, 25).
This repeated phrase tells us that God put limits upon each species
and generic class. However, there is room for change and adaptation

to environment within each kind. Is this all that is meant by evolution? Is that what Charles Darwin taught when he published *Origin of the Species*, over one hundred years ago? It most certainly is not! Evolution, as a scientific framework of thought, means much more than horizontal change. Evolution is a philosophy of life that touches every arena of intellectual pursuit.

Evolution asserts that life forms are moving from the simple to the complex, onward and upward, from protoplasm to paradise! Sir Julian Huxley, the world-renowned British biologist, has emphasized the all-inclusive nature of evolutionary thought:

> The concept of evolution was soon extended into other than biological fields. Inorganic subjects such as life-histories of stone and the formation of the chemical elements on the one hand, and on the other hand subjects like linguistics, social anthropology, and comparative law and religion, began to be studied from the evolutionary angle, until today we are enabled to see evolution as a universal and all-pervading process.[2]

Notice Dr. Huxley's phrase, ". . . a universal and all-pervading process." A few pages later, Huxley proclaims almost fanatically:

> Furthermore, with the adoption of the evolutionary approach in non-biological fields, from cosmology to human affairs, we are beginning to realize that biological evolution is only one aspect of evolution in general. Evolution in the extended sense can be defined as a directional and essentially irreversible process occurring in time, which in its course gives rise to an increase of variety and an increasingly high level of organization in its products. Our present knowledge indeed forces us to the view that the whole of reality *is* evolution—a single process of self-transformation.[3]

Huxley has made his mark on twentieth-century thought perhaps more than his grandfather, Thomas Huxley, did in the nineteenth century. Now, if evolution is what he claims it to be, then evolution has taken the place of God Himself! As he said, ". . . the whole of reality *is* evolution . . . ." Only as far back as 1960, Huxley stated:

> Darwinism removed the whole idea of God as the creator of organisms from the sphere of rational discussion. Darwin pointed out that no supernatural designer was needed; since natural selection could account for any known form of life, there was no room for a supernatural agency in its evolution . . . . There was no sudden moment during evolutionary history when "spirit" was instilled into life, any more than there was a single moment when it was instilled into you . . . . I think we can dismiss entirely all idea of a supernatural overriding mind being responsible for the evolutionary process.[4]

An Exalted Position

If you think Sir Julian has stretched the truth a bit, let me assure you—he has! Yet, his evaluation of evolution as the whole of reality is creedal truth to the vast majority of the scientific community.

In May 1979 the Smithsonian Institute spent many thousands of dollars on a massive display on evolution. When asked by a reporter as to the value of such a program, the head curator said it was worthwhile "because evolution is the basis of all thought." Evolutionary thought does touch all the disciplines. Sigmund Freud applied Darwin's hypothesis to psychology, and he explained away belief in God. Freud saw man's universal belief in God as the evolutionary outgrowth of primitive man's fear of his alien environment. Thus, to overcome fear of nature, man invented his gods to protect him. As man progressed onward and upward, his ideas became more refined, until his primitive gods became civilized and even fraternalized; the highest evolved thought being Jesus' concept of our "heavenly Father." Of course, as Freud observed, God is not really *there,* except in our minds. This philosophy was confirmed when Henry W. Brosin, chairman of the Department of Psychiatry at the University of Pittsburgh, said:

It is appropriate for psychiatrists and other students of mental disorders to pay homage to the work of Charles Robert Darwin and the theory of evolution, for without this work it is difficult to imagine what the state of our discipline would be like.[5]

This kind of thinking gave birth to German Rationalism, a century ago, which nearly destroyed Europe's and America's faith in the Bible as God's inspired Word. Those nineteenth-century theologians took Darwin's "truth" and applied it to biblical studies and managed to remove the supernatural from the Scriptures, until there was very little left that could be called God's Word. Liberalism, which has its roots in evolutionary philosophy, began to tell us that Moses did not get his creation story from heaven, but rather from Persia! In fact, Moses didn't receive it at all. Therefore, Genesis is merely primitive myth and much too unsophisticated to tell us anything of value about *how* God created the universe. Of course, evolution can explain it, and without any reference to God.

The current textbook used by my teenage son in a high-school biology class says of the creation of life:

> The atmosphere was made up of gases such as ammonia, methane, and water vapor. Energy from lightning or radiation split up some of these molecules. The elements carbon, hydrogen, nitrogen and oxygen then bonded in new combinations as organic molecules. Finally, the right organic molecules came together in the right way and life began.[6]

In fact, evolution can explain almost anything. One only has to examine the writings of the experts in all the natural and social sciences to become aware of the broad outreach of evolutionary theory. In astronomy and cosmology, for example, it is nearly universally believed that everything in the universe has gradually evolved. For example we read:

> We should expect to find stars and galaxies in all stages of evolution as they form from existing material and then de-

cay. For stars this is certainly the case . . . . There may be
a similar evolutionary process for galaxies, but at the moment we do not have enough experimental evidence to give
us the clues to the evolutionary pattern.[7]

This last statement makes us wonder where the scientist obtains
experimental evidence on the evolution of galaxies!

If evolution were merely a scientific theory affecting only the interpretation of the data of biology, geology, and astronomy, then we
would not need to be too concerned about it. If evolutionary history
could be harmonized with the biblical revelation of creation in some
satisfactory way, then most Christians would be content to leave the
subject to the scientist and not concern themselves about it.
However, this is not the case. Evolutionary philosophy lies at the
very heart of the public-school system in America.

A good example of the far-reaching influence of this idea
in America is the fact that practically the entire structure of
modern public school education is centered around this
theme. This fact is so obvious and so common to universal
observation and experience that it needs no documentation.

The evolutionary origin of the universe, of life and of man
is taught as scientific fact even to elementary school children in probably most public schools, at least by implica-
tion. The Christian and Biblical record of origins is usually
ignored, sometimes allegorized or even ridiculed. Such con-
cepts as Creation, the Fall, the Curse, Sin, Redemption,
etc.—which really are the most important and basic facts of
science and history—are taboo. Such patronizing references
to "religion" as are allowed at all in the public schools are
given in a context of comparative religions of "world com-
munities," of "brotherhood," of "social progress," and the
like.

This is a remarkable phenomenon in a nation founded on
Christianity and the Bible. Undoubtedly, many factors have
contributed to this "devolution," but it is highly probable
that the introduction of the 19th-century doctrines of
evolutionary optimism is back of most of it." [8]

John Dewey is recognized as the founder of the American public-school movement. It is significant that Dewey was entirely evolutionary in his philosophy. This philosophy, based on biology, saw man as a part of his environment. The surroundings in which man existed remade man, Dewey believed, as well as man remaking them. Dewey felt that man's origins and functions alone, apart from anything supernatural, could lead to understanding him.

A Compromise

What has been the result of this widespread acceptance of evolution as scientific fact? One of the tragic results is that the church decided it needed to incorporate and "baptize" Darwin. The rise of religious modernism at the end of the last century had its roots in Darwinism. Theologians became convinced of the truth of evolution and therefore felt compelled to seek a compromise between Scripture and evolution. Theologians accepted the long geological ages and the evolution of species, including man. It then became mandatory for various schemes to be worked out for harmonizing the creation account, in Genesis, and evolutionary thought. We shall examine these different theories a bit later, but suffice it to say that none of them have been valid. The end result has been a complete rejection of Genesis by many as only myth and legend.

> Thus the Genesis account of creation and the fall is rejected as history—as most of us understand history. Science, the Barthians say, has delivered us from having to believe the Genesis stories, and through this scientific deliverance, we are supposed to be able to see the real meaning of the accounts.[9]

A Sacred Cow

The tension I am made to feel is that I don't want to make the Bible say what I want it to say. I don't want to make the Holy Scriptures fit in an evolutionary scheme. Yet, in the minds of many, it is sheer folly to attack the credibility of evolution. As Huxley and others have stated repeatedly, "All intelligent persons agree that evolution is a fact." However, having spent many hours discussing this subject with hundreds of people, I am convinced that the reason most educated people believe in evolution is simply because they have been told that most educated people believe in evolution! Well, as the author of this book, I do not believe in evolution, and I am a well-educated person! I have some very valid reasons for rejecting evolution, and I'd like to explain them to you. The reader will be surprised at how easy it is to topple this sacred cow off its throne. It is a rather simple matter to demonstrate that evolution is not only antibiblical, but also totally unscientific.

Genesis and Evolution

First of all, can Genesis be harmonized with the evolutionary explanation of origins? I think not, and for several obvious reasons. To begin with, several attempted compromises just fail to answer some important questions. The first attempt, to say that God used evolution as His method of Creation, is called Theistic Evolution. This approach says Genesis 1:1: "In the beginning God created the heavens and the earth," explains the idea of first cause. That is, behind the evolutionary process is God, who "started the ball rolling," and evolution was the method He used; the rest of Genesis 1 is poetry and says nothing of the *how* of creation. Can a thinking Christian accept this explanation? Well, I tried it for a while, and it didn't satisfy me. Why? First of all it gives too much away to evolution as *the* factual method of creation. As far back as I can remember, evolution has always left two questions unanswered for me. How did the process get started (first cause), and where is the evidence for transmigration of species? The first question is answered for the theist who believes Genesis 1:1, which tells us God is the First Cause. We, as Christians, can and do believe that. The atheistic evolutionist has no answer to this question, because he wasn't there in the beginning of time and can't demonstrate how nothing evolved into something. The evolutionist is equally hard put to demonstrate how one species "transmigrates" into another totally different species. Nowhere in the scientific world is there evidence of such a transition. There are no "missing links" of half-forms, caught in the long line of evolutionary process.[10] This is what I mean when I say Theistic Evolution gives too much credit to evolution as fact.

Why Some Christians Accept Evolution

Many Christians don't want to seem unscientific, so they feel some compromise between evolution and the Scriptures is necessary.

Dr. James Coppedge has listed three reasons why some believers have accepted Theistic Evolution:

- Scientists can easily overestimate the supposed evidences of evolution outside their particular field. A physicist, for example, may be persuaded that the biologists have real proof of evolution, and as a scientist he respects the reports of other scientists.

  Many professional people, including scientists in other specialties, may be mistakenly led to believe that the scientists have proved evolution to be true, and they have to do the best they can with it. Doing the best they can, in such a case, they espouse the idea that God did it, but through gradual, natural processes.
- Some believers in God are not clearly aware that the Bible and evolution are not compatible. They suppose that Theistic Evolution is a philosophy acceptable to the Christian faith, not having thought through the contradiction involved. Among these are some great souls who started out as unbelievers and have gotten as far as faith in God, but have not yet encountered or fully considered the Bible's teachings on this subject.
- Difficulties with the "geologic time scale," descriptions of early man, and astronomers' recounting the vastness of the universe—these may lead one to an unadvisable reinterpretation of the Bible account.[11]

Progressive Creationism

Another attempt to reconcile evolution and Genesis is what Dr. Bernard Ramm called Progressive Creationism.[12] As a college student, I once thought this solution was creditable. What this idea says is that God started the process of creation (Genesis 1:1) then used horizontal evolution within each species. Then after centuries of change and adaption within each kind, God would intervene and create again. Each act of creation (with millions of years in between) would introduce higher and more complex forms of life. Thus the ape was followed by pre-man and pre-man by man. This explanation is attractive because it answers the two questions of first cause and the missing links. It answers the question of first cause in that it postulates God as creator. It answers why there are no missing links in that God created each species "after its kind," with no transitional forms or vertical evolution in between. Progressive Creationism allows for six literal days (twenty-four hours) of creation, but not six successive days and a literal week. Progressive Creationism is a very attractive theory and has many followers. However, after much thought, I have found that there are problems with this theory. Does this theory harmonize with evolution? Only on the surface. If we look closely at what Genesis 1 says, we immediately recognize a problem. Did you ever notice that the chronology of days is wrong in Genesis, if we try to harmonize it with evolution?

LIGHT WITHOUT THE SUN. Genesis 1:3–5 describes how God said, "Let there be light," and the light came; and He named the light *day,* and the darkness He called *night.* Genesis then says, ". . . And there was evening and there was morning, one day" (Genesis 1:5). I believe this was a literal, twenty-four-hour day, or one rotation of the earth on its axis, as it was exposed to the sun. Genesis then describes the creation of the plant kingdom on the third day. Now comes a remarkable statement. Genesis 1:14–19 tells us that on the fourth day God created the sun, the moon, and the stars. The question that arises, for any scientist, is: "How can you have a twenty-four-hour day (on the first *day*), when the sun has not yet been created?" Furthermore how can you have the creation of plant life without the sun? Photosynthesis must take place for there to be plant life. So you see, even if God *did* create in six literal days of creation with millions of years in between, how could the plant kingdom exist for millions of years without the sun for its life source? Therefore, if Progressive Creationism was indeed God's method of creation, it creates a tremendous problem for science. It must explain millions of years of plant life, photosynthesis, and evolutionary progress, all without the sun! Admittedly, this is a difficult hypothesis, [13] so the Day-Age Theory of Progressive Creationism creates as many problems as it solves. Thomas Huxley said many years ago: "It is clear that the doctrine of evolution is directly antagonistic to that of creation . . . evolution, if consistently accepted, makes it impossible to believe the Bible." [14]

Some writers have observed that this problem is solved when we do not require a literal interpretation of the creation narrative in Genesis. They have said that since Genesis is merely a religious poem, we shouldn't expect details of the narrative to be scientific. This sounds good on the surface, but it just does not hold water. If Genesis is inspired of God, then, whether it is allegory, poetry, or what have you, it still should be *correct* poetry or allegory. In other words, if God wrote it, then He would know that the sun had to be there for evolution to take place. He would know that the sun must exist before biological life can continue. For God to have inspired someone to write it incorrectly violates any valid concept of divine inspiration. Granted, much of Scripture is prescientific, but even when Scriptures do not address themselves to scientific matters, they still speak true science. It is the conviction of many outstanding scientific minds that Genesis 1 is true science and is reliable as a source of information on origins.

CREATION IN SIX DAYS. Is it reasonable that God really created the world in six, consecutive, twenty-four-hour days of a literal week? What about all the evidence for the great antiquity of the earth and life forms? How does evolution fit into such an interpretation? These are worthy questions and ones that many conservative, Bible-believing Christians have struggled with. The conclusion that I have come to, after years of study, is that if we take Genesis seriously, as real history and not as parable, then evolution cannot be true history. Genesis 1 and other related Bible passages that deal with creation can never be made to coincide with the theory of evolution.

THE "DAYS" OF CREATION. If we are to take linguistics seriously, as a science, then we must listen to its conclusions. Genesis uses the Hebrew word for "day" repeatedly. This word is *yom*. When used in the singular, *yom* in the Old Testament always means a literal, twenty-four-hour period of time. It never means an age or era of time. For example, the Old Testament prophets often speak of the great "day [*yom*] of the Lord." This means a literal day when the Lord shall come. It will be followed by an era of messianic rule, but it begins with the day He comes. Notice that Genesis tells us that God called the newly created light *yom* (Genesis 1:5), and the verse says there was a morning and an evening, one day (*yom*) then a second day (*yom*), and a third. Now that's rather specific. That doesn't sound like allegory to me. This is a clear description of the earth spinning on its axis.[15]

SPECIFIC DAYS. Notice further that Genesis tells us that after each day's work God called His work "good." His creative work was good, full, and complete. There is no survival of the fittest, no death and decay, all of which are necessary if God's method was evolution. What is "good" about the evolutionary process? Bondage, death, decay, and struggle are evil, not good, in God's world. God's method was good: no death and struggle. Also, we are told that God was very specific in what He created. Ten times it is said that God created each species and life form "after its kind" (Genesis 1:21–25). The Genesis account of creation is very plain in saying that individual varieties in basic kinds may be possible, but only within God's predescribed limits. God created the kinds, or species, each fully developed, a restriction which would preclude real evolution. Each kind was created with the appearance of age; thus Adam and Eve were created as adults, not as evolving life forms.

A LITERAL WEEK. Again, Genesis states that, at the conclusion of the creation period, God ceased His creative work. "And by the seventh day God completed His work which He had done; and He rested on the seventh day from all His work which He had done" (Genesis 2:2). These words tell us another direct contradiction between Genesis and the evolutionary theory of origins. Genesis 2 tells us that the processes of the creation period of six days are no longer working; they ceased. The processes that God used to create *all* things are no longer in operation. This fact is stated again in the Ten Commandments (Exodus 20:11). Then, centuries later, the Holy

Spirit inspired the writer of Hebrews to affirm the same truth, ". . . although His works were finished from the foundation of the world . . . . and God rested on the seventh day from all His works" (Hebrews 4:3, 4). This is not what evolution affirms. Darwin's theory would have us believe that the creative processes are going on continuously, creating new species, and so on throughout the past and into the future. The Word of God says *no!* God's original creation took only six days, less than one week, and He "finished" His work. When God rested, He looked out upon a completed creation, not a process of struggle for survival. He saw man, a completed creature made in His own image. He saw each living form complete "after its kind." His creation was good, complete, and He "rested."

An Obvious Conclusion

It seems obvious to me that Genesis does not teach evolution. Anyone who tries to reconcile these two very different statements about origins just isn't being honest about the very real problems. The conclusion is simple: Somebody's mistaken! Either evolution is wrong or Genesis is wrong; you can't have it both ways. If you stand on the side of evolution, the whole of biblical inspiration stands in judgment. It will not do to call the Genesis narrative of creation a parable or poem. This is scholastic dishonesty. Let it say what it says, and decide if it is true. So great is the problem, that Dr. Henry Morris has noted over twenty contradictions between Genesis and modern geology.[16]

Genesis—Science or Pre-Science

Because these many contradictions exist, a popular conclusion is that the creation narratives are pre-science and say nothing about the *how* of creation. Some theologians have decided that we must read Genesis to find the *who* of creation, and then read *National Geographic* to discover the *how.* However, there is a strong fellowship of men and women in the scientific fraternity who view Genesis as real history. These *creationists* see creation as true science. Perhaps the man who has championed this position more than any other is Dr. Henry Morris, director of the Institute for Creation

Research.[17] Dr. Morris and his colleagues argue that evolutionary theory is nonscience, because it cannot be demonstrated scientifically. I know this sounds ridiculous, when we consider the fact that evolution is seen by nearly all men of science as the *only* real science of origins. Yet, creationists have a very strong case against evolution. The purpose of this chapter is to show that evolution was not and is not God's method of creation. The best way of doing this is by stating the case for creation and the case against evolution. Creationists reject evolution for many reasons, but their strongest argument comes from the First and Second Laws of Thermodynamics. Dr. Morris has observed repeatedly in his books and lectures that the creation accounts in Genesis entirely agree with these two laws of science, while evolution contradicts them completely. These two laws of thermodynamics are the foundation stones upon which all real science is built. Anything that contradicts them is nonscience.

THE LAWS OF THERMODYNAMICS. What are these two laws of nature? What do they say? The First Law of Thermodynamics has to do with the conservation of energy. Energy may be defined as "the capacity to do work." Actually, it includes everything in the physical universe. We know that the material world is merely forms of energy. What then is the First Law of Energy?

"The First Law of Thermodynamics is merely another name for the Law of Conservation of Energy . . . This law states that energy can be transformed in various ways, but can neither be created nor destroyed." [18] This then is the first law of the universe. All processes in the universe, regardless of their nature, involve the transformation of energy. All of these processes work within the limits of the law of energy conservation, which states that mass energy is neither being created nor destroyed.

THE BIBLE AND THE FIRST LAW OF THERMODYNAMICS. How does the biblical revelation stand up against this first law of nature? It confirms it. The writer of Genesis stated the principle of the first law centuries before man even heard the word *science*. According to Scripture, creation took place in time past, and is no longer taking place.

Thus the heavens and the earth were completed, and all their hosts. And by the seventh day God completed His work which He had done; and He rested on the seventh day from all His work which He had done. Then God blessed the seventh day and sanctified it, because in it He rested from all His work which God had created and made.

Genesis 2:1–3

For in six days the Lord made the heavens and the earth, the sea and all that is in them, and rested on the seventh day; therefore the Lord blessed the sabbath day and made it holy.

Exodus 20:11

It is a sign between Me and the sons of Israel forever; for in six days the Lord made heaven and earth, but on the seventh day He ceased from labor, and was refreshed.

Exodus 31:17

By the word of the Lord the heavens were made. And by the breath of His mouth all their host. He gathers the waters of the sea together as a heap; He lays up the deeps in storehouses. Let all the earth fear the Lord; Let all the inhabitants of the world stand in awe of Him. For He spoke, and it was done; He commanded, and it stood fast.

Psalms 33:6–9

Thou alone art the Lord. Thou has made the heavens. The heaven of heavens with all their host, The earth and all that is on it, The seas and all that is in them. Thou dost give life to all of them And the heavenly host bows down before Thee.

Nehemiah 9:6

For when they maintain this, it escapes their notice that by the word of God the heavens existed long ago and the earth was formed out of water and by water.

2 Peter 3:5

For we who have believed enter that rest, just as He has
said, "As I swore in My wrath, They shall not enter My
rest," although His works were finished from the foundation
of the world.

Hebrews 4:3

For the one who has entered His rest has himself also
rested from his works, as God did from His.

Hebrews 4:10

These marvelously accurate passages speak true science in that they
tell us two things: God created everything in six days, and He is no
longer creating anything; second, He is preserving everything He
created.

God has, therefore, told us plainly in His word that nothing is now being either created or destroyed, and we are,
therefore, not surprised when, as we study the laws of nature, we find that the most basic, the most universal, the
best-proved, law of all science is the law of Conservation! [19]

EVOLUTION AND THE FIRST LAW. At this point it ought to be evi-
dent that evolutionary theory directly contradicts this universal law
of energy conservation. Evolution asserts that *creation* is a continuing process, in that there is increasing organization and integration
and development taking place in the present. This philosophy, called
"uniformitarianism" [20] states that all present biological processes
have taken place in the past, *uniformly*. It states that the present is
the key for the past. Lest there be any doubt that evolutionists teach
this on-going, ever-upward complexity of life forms, consider the
words of Sir Julian Huxley again:

Evolution is a one-way process, irreversible in time,
producing apparent novelties and greater variety, and leading to higher degrees of organization, more differentiated,
more complex, but at the same time more integrated.[21]

However, there is no evidence that such a process described by
evolutionists is now taking place anywhere in the world. According

to Scripture, this process is called "creation," and it is no longer taking place. According to the science of the First Law, it cannot take place on a vertical, upward scale of complexity.

EVOLUTION AND THE SECOND LAW. Because evolutionary theory violates the First Law of Thermodynamics, what can we say about its relationship to the Second Law? This universal law of science has to do with the transference of energy from one state, or condition, to another. The Second Law was originally developed by Nicholas Carnot, Rudolf Clausius, and William Kelvin, as they worked with problems relating to steam engines, about the time Darwin was publishing his *Origin of Species*. It has taken many years for this law to be recognized for its implications concerning evolutionary thought. What then is this Second Law? A noted physicist says, concerning the two laws of thermodynamics:

> Thermodynamics is a physical theory of great generality impinging on practically every phase of human experience. It may be called the description of the behaviour of matter in equilibrium and of its changes from one equilibrium state to another. Thermodynamics operates with two master concepts or constructs and two great principles. The concepts are energy and entropy, and the principles are the so-called first and second laws of thermodynamics . . . .[22]

These laws affect all of the physical universe, including the biological world. The Second Law basically says everything is running down, growing old, becoming more "probable." Princeton biologist Harold Blum, applying the Second Law to biological systems says:

> A major consequence of the second law of thermodynamics is that all real processes go toward a condition of greatest probability. The probability function generally used in thermodynamics is entropy . . . . The second law of thermodynamics says that left to itself any isolated system will go toward greater entropy, which also means toward greater randomization and greater likelihood.[23]

This, then, is the second law of science. It says all clocks are running down, all babies are growing old, all systems are wearing out. Everything in the universe is increasing in entropy, moving toward disorganization, randomization, and a decrease in complexity. Evolution says just the opposite is true. As Huxley defined it, evolution involves a continual, upward increase in order and complexity. Now, friends, these two opposite principles cannot both be true. There is absolutely no scientific doubt that the Second Law of Thermodynamics is true! But where does that leave evolutionary theory? Evolutionists have argued in vain against this comparison, by suggesting that entropy may decrease in an "open" system. For example, a child is born and grows to adulthood. A skyscraper is designed and built—an increase in organization and a decrease in entropy. They say this allows for evolution to develop from simple life forms to complex life forms. Not so, says the Second Law. Any such growth in complexity is only a temporary thing, due to an increase in energy. However, everything in the universe will eventually grow old and die. "Even the temporary, supposedly natural growth of an organism is really to be attributed alternately to the creation and maintenance by God of a marvelous mechanism of reproduction and sustenance." [24]

THE BIBLE AND THE SECOND LAW. The evolutionist has an unanswered question here, but what about the Bible? Is its philosophy compatible with the Second Law? absolutely. The Second Law is merely a modern, scientific expression of what the Scriptures describe as the Fall and the Curse. The Bible tells us that because of Adam's sin in the garden, the whole of nature is cursed by death and decay. Romans 8:22 says: "For we know that the whole creation groans and suffers the pains of childbirth together until now." Jesus himself said it well, "Heaven and earth will pass away . . ." (Matthew 24:35). As a Christian I find this very exciting. Ages ago, God's Word explained the basic laws of energy to us. The Bible tells us that God created everything, then finished His creation; and He is now preserving what He made. This is the Law of Conservation of Energy. Then the Scriptures explain that God's created world had no death or decay until man's rebellion and sin. Man turned God's good creation into a nightmare. ". . . through one man sin entered into the world, and death through sin . . ." (Romans 5:12). Thus the Fall began the Second Law; the law of entropy increase. Thus God's Word is scientifically true, while evolutionary theory stands judged and undemonstrated experimentally, historically, or scientifically.

What About the Evidence for Evolution?

Perhaps the reader desires further study on this subject and feels this chapter has been too simplistic. Those who have a background of evolutionary training no doubt have many questions to ask. How about the fossil record and the geology which prove the great antiquity of this planet and give evidence of evolution? It is beyond the scope of this chapter to disprove evolution. My purpose has been only to show that Scripture does not teach evolution. I personally am convinced that evolution is the devil's lie and cannot be demonstrated scientifically or otherwise. The Bible does give explanations that are valid for those who are willing to consider its claims.[25] The real harm comes when unthinking Christians seek a halfway-house philosophy by seeking to join a godless, materialistic philosophy with the teachings of God's Word. Further study can only convince the thinking Christian that this clearly is not possible. Also it is not what God describes to us. Evolution does not make men out of monkeys; it only makes monkeys out of men! Let's not let evolutionary theory make monkeys out of Christians. "Study to show thyself approved . . ." (2 Timothy 2:15 KJV).

Source Notes

1. Henry M. Morris, *The Twilight of Evolution* (Grand Rapids, MI: Baker Book House, 1963), pp. 1, 2.
2. James R. Newman, "Evolution and Genetics," *What Is Science?* (NY: Simon and Schuster, 1955), p. 272.
3. Ibid., p. 278.
4. Sol Tax and Charles Callender, eds., "At Random: A Television Preview," *Issues in Evolution*, Vol. 3. *Evolution After Darwin* (Chicago: University of Chicago Press, 1960), p. 41.
5. Sol Tax and Charles Callender, eds., "Evolution and Understanding Diseases of the Mind," *Evolution of Man: Man, Culture, and Society*, Vol. 2. *Evolution After Darwin* (Chicago: University of Chicago Press, 1960), p. 373.
6. James H. Otto and Albert Towle, *Modern Biology* (NY: Holt, Rinehart and Winston, 1977), pp. 149, 150.
7. Gerald S. Hawkins, "A New Theory of the Universe," *Science Digest* 52 (November 1962), 45.
8. Henry M. Morris, *The Twilight of Evolution*, pp. 19, 20.
9. Charles Ryrie, *Neo-Orthodoxy* (Chicago: Moody Press, 1956), p. 51.
10. The evolutionist often cites the reptilelike bird *Archaeopteryx* as an example of a transitional form. However, knowledgeable scientific creationists, as well as many evolutionists, are very skeptical about this creature as being a "missing link." See Duane Gish, *Evolution? The Fossils Say No* (San Diego: Creation-Life Pubns., 1973).
11. James Coppedge, *Evolution: Possible or Impossible?* (Grand Rapids, MI: Zondervan, 1973), p. 177.
12. Bernard Ramm, *The Christian View of Science and the Scripture.* (Grand Rapids, MI: Wm. B. Eerdmans, 1954).
13. Among those who allow for a Day-Age type theory is James Reid. Mr. Reid has a good discussion of how it might have been possible for there to be life forms, and so on, without the sun. *See* chapter entitled "The God of the 'Dark' Sun" in Reid's book *God, the Atom and the Universe* (Grand Rapids, MI: Zondervan, 1968), pp. 125 ff.

14. Fred John Meldau, *Why We Believe in Creation, Not in Evolution* (Denver: Christian Victory Pub., 1959), p. 8.

15. *See* Henry Morris, *Biblical Cosmology and Modern Science* (Nutley, NJ: Presbyterian and Reformed Pub. Co., 1970), pp. 58, 59. These pages have a good discussion of the Day-Age Theory and the biblical use of the Hebrew/ word *yom*.

16. Ibid., pp. 59–62.

17. Henry M. Morris is the director of the Institute for Creation Research, American Heritage College, San Diego, CA. A noted professor and scientist, Dr. Morris has written many books refuting evolution, some of which are listed in this chapter's Additional Reading.

18. A. R. Ubbelohde, *Man and Energy* (NY: George Braziller, Inc., 1955), p. 149.

19. Henry Morris, *The Twilight of Evolution*, p. 32.

20. Sir Charles Lyell (1797–1875) has been called the "high priest of uniformitarianism." His famous textbook, *Elements of Geology*, was a great influence on Charles Darwin. Indeed Darwin could not have formulated the theory of evolution without the principle of uniformitarianism, as he openly admitted.

21. Sol Tax and Charles Callender, eds., "At Random: A Television Preview," *Issues in Evolution*, Vol. 3, *Evolution After Darwin* (Chicago: University of Chicago Press, 1975), p. 44.

22. R. B. Lindsay, "Entropy Consumption and Values in Physical Science," *American Scientist* 41 (September 1959), 376.

23. Harold Blum, "Perspectives in Evolution," *American Scientist* 43 (October 1955), 595.

24. Henry M. Morris, *The Twilight of Evolution*, p. 35.

25. All of antiquity, the fossil record, and other "evidences" of evolution can better be explained in terms of: the Creation, the Fall, the Curse, and the Universal Flood. As Dr. John Whitcomb had said, ". . . a true historical geology will never be formulated until the Genesis flood, as a universal aqueous catastrophe, is granted its rightful and vital place in the thinking of Christian men of science."

Additional Reading

Coppedge, James. *Evolution: Possible or Impossible?* Grand Rapids, MI: Zondervan, 1973.

Davidheiser, Bolton. *Evolution and Christian Faith.* Nutley, NJ: Presbyterian and Reformed Pub. Co., 1969.

Filby, Fredrick A. *The Flood Reconsidered.* Grand Rapids, MI: Zondervan, 1970.

Morris, Henry M. *Biblical Cosmology and Modern Science.* Nutley, NJ: Presbyterian and Reformed Pub. Co., 1970.

Morris, Henry M. *Evolution and the Modern Christian.* Nutley, NJ: Presbyterian and Reformed Pub. Co., 1967.

Morris, Henry M. *The Twilight of Evolution.* Grand Rapids: MI: Baker Book House, 1963.

Reid, James. *God, the Atom and the Universe.* Grand Rapids, MI: Zondervan, 1968.

Schaeffer, Francis A. *Genesis in Space and Time.* Downers Grove, IL: Inter-Varsity Press, 1972.

Whitcomb, John C., Jr., and Morris, Henry M. *The Genesis Flood.* Nutley, NJ: Presbyterian and Reformed Pub. Co., 1961.